THE NATURAL PROZAC PROGRAM

The *NATURAL* PROZAC PROGRAM

How to Use St. John's Wort, the Antidepressant Herb

JONATHAN ZUESS, M.D.

THREE RIVERS PRESS

New York

Published by Three Rivers Press, a division of Crown Publishers, Inc., 201 East 50th Street, New York, NY 10022. Member of the Crown Publishing Group.

Random House, Inc. New York, Toronto, London, Sydney, Auckland

http://www.randomhouse.com/

THREE RIVERS PRESS and colophon are trademarks of Crown Publishers, Inc.

Design by Susan Hood

Printed in the United States of America

Library of Congress Cataloging-in-Publication Data
Zuess, Jonathan.
    The natural Prozac program : how to use St. John's wort, the antidepressant herb / by Jonathan Zuess. — 1st U.S. ed.
        p.   cm.
    Includes bibliographical references.
    1. Depression, Mental—Alternative treatment. 2. Hypericum perforatum—Therapeutic use. I. Title.
RC537.Z84 1997
616.85′27061—dc21   97-8064
                                                      CIP

ISBN 0-609-80152-X

10 9 8 7 6 5 4 3 2 1

First Edition

CONTENTS

the brain's feel-good chemicals • Boosting the immune system

Appendixes

ACKNOWLEDGMENTS

I give my thanks to the following people for their assistance in the creation of this book: William Couldwell, M.D., Ph.D., of the University of North Dakota's Trinity Medical Center; Daniel Meruelo, Ph.D., of the New York University Medical Center; the U.S. Department of Agriculture; Ron Chord, organic farmer at the Flower Mountain Farm in Washington State; Ted Snider, farm manager at the Eclectic Institute in Oregon; Sarah Jane Freymann at the Stepping Stone Literary Agency; and Leslie Meredith and Laura Wood at Harmony Books. Finally, I'd also like to thank all of my many other teachers—they know who they are.

IMPORTANT NOTICE

This book is not intended for use as a substitute for consultation with a qualified medical practitioner. If you have symptoms of depression, it is essential that you see your doctor immediately. You are unique, and your diagnosis and treatment must be individualized for you by your own doctor.

This book provides exciting information about St. John's wort, but no book can provide the personalized care that you need. As with any potent medicine, your doctor should be involved in your decision to use St. John's wort.

The author or his agents will not accept responsibility for injury, loss, or damage occasioned to any person acting or refraining from action as a result of material in this book, whether or not such injury, loss, or damage is due in any way to any negligent act or omission, breach of duty, or default on the part of the author or his agents.

For the sake of privacy, the names of the patients whose stories are told in this book, and the personal details that might identify them, have been changed.

The author has no financial interest in any producer or supplier of St. John's wort.

Introduction

ST. JOHN'S WORT—
BETTER THAN PROZAC

Almost every one of us experiences the symptoms of depression at some time in our lives. Our minds, bodies, and spirits can't always adjust to the stressful and toxic lifestyles that we've come to consider normal in the late twentieth century. And yet, the treatments we've used for depression—like Prozac, Tofranil, and dozens of other synthetic drugs—are seriously toxic in themselves, adding to the overload on our bodies. Now, we know of a natural alternative.

Exciting new studies in prestigious medical journals have shown us that the herb St. John's wort (or *Hypericum*), used for thousands of years by the "wise women" herbalists of Europe and Asia, is *as effective as the best of modern drugs* for the treatment of mild depression. It is also effective in treating premenstrual syndrome (PMS), anxiety, chronic insomnia, and a host of other conditions. But most amazing of all, it has extraordinarily few side effects.

Medical researchers have been astonished to discover that

even though St. John's wort works as well as antidepressant drugs like Prozac and Tofranil, it has only a fraction of the number of side effects that they do. It is far gentler on the system. It doesn't cause drowsiness or interact with alcohol. Nor does it interfere with the ability to concentrate or dream like other antidepressants. In fact, tests show that St. John's wort actually enhances the brain's problem-solving abilities. This means it nurtures the body/mind's own emotional healing response, instead of suppressing it as drugs often do. To top it all off, it's much cheaper than other antidepressants.

Put simply, St. John's wort beats Prozac hands down.

Sometimes conventional antidepressant drugs really are necessary—as in cases of severe or treatment-resistant depression. On the other hand, though, most people who have depression are only *mildly* depressed. Yet many doctors still prescribe toxic drugs like Prozac for them, because they believe they have no alternative.

Today, St. John's wort is establishing itself as that much-needed alternative. Doctors in Europe have already come to rely on it. In 1993 alone, for instance, German doctors wrote over 2.7 *million* prescriptions for it.

In *The Natural Prozac Program* you'll learn all about St. John's wort: where it comes from, how it works, how to buy and use it, and the results you can expect. You'll read about the breakthrough scientific studies that have established it as one of the hottest new treatments in all of medicine. And you'll trace its roots deep into the traditions of the ancient herbalists.

Is St. John's wort right for you?

THE NATURAL PROZAC PROGRAM

Chapter 1

HOW ST. JOHN'S WORT CAN HELP YOU

In the crumbling pages of ancient texts on healing, hidden amongst the dusty basement shelves of a neglected Old World library, there are stories of a flower whose tears are magical. These bright red tears, it was said, have the power to ward off all manner of illness and misfortune. According to ancient teaching, however, the tears or drops could only be gathered once a year, on a holy day in midsummer, when the flowers bloomed with a brief and startling brilliance.

There really is such a medicinal plant, and its flowers really do have an extraordinary healing power. St. John's wort is as effective for healing depression as any other medication known, but it is virtually free of side effects. It can also heal anxiety disorders, PMS, and insomnia.

Let me introduce you to Elaine, one of the growing number of people who have discovered the seeming magic of St. John's wort for themselves.

Elaine's Story

Elaine had begun to think that nothing was going to help her feel any better. For months, she'd had low-level feelings of depression and anxiety that were making her life more and more difficult. She had tried several different medications, but none of them seemed to agree with her. Until she tried St. John's wort.

Elaine was lucky—she had a good doctor. He kept up with the journals, and had read about the latest studies on a powerful antidepressant medication with virtually no side effects: St. John's wort. He had also read that it has been used safely for thousands of years, and that today it is one of the antidepressants most often prescribed by European family doctors and psychiatrists. Although Elaine was skeptical about herbs, she agreed to give St. John's wort a try.

Elaine took a few drops of the liquid extract in a glass of water each morning and evening. That's all there was to it. In the first week, the most significant thing that she noticed was, quite simply, *nothing*. There were no side effects from it, like she'd had from all the synthetic drugs she'd tried. No light-headedness, like she'd gotten from Prozac. No blurry vision or difficulty concentrating, like Tofranil had given her. And no stomach upset, as she'd had with Zoloft.

And then, around the eighth day, she started to feel its therapeutic effects. She had her first good night's sleep in months. Her flu that had been dragging on for weeks suddenly cleared up, and her energy level improved, giving her a sense of physical well-being.

Over the next six weeks on St. John's wort, her irritability and depression gradually disappeared. Sure, she still had the occasional rough day at work, but she felt calmer, more able to control her anxiety and mood upsets, and could more easily get her mind out of the pattern of worrying about trivial things. In fact, she was able to concentrate even better than before.

Today, six months after starting St. John's wort, Elaine is still doing great. She's had no relapse of her symptoms, and has had absolutely no side effects. She's switched to a low dose—just a few drops in her juice in the mornings. This is how hundreds of thousands of Europeans use it every day.

Elaine is just one of the increasingly large group of people who've discovered how effective and safe St. John's wort is. More and more doctors are prescribing it, and with the many top-quality studies that have come out in the last few years, chances are that it will eventually be more widely used than Prozac. In fact, because it has been used for thousands of years by herbal healers around the world, it is probably already the most-used antidepressant in the history of humanity. As you'll discover in this book, St. John's wort really is *natural Prozac.*

Who Will Benefit from Using St. John's Wort?

St. John's wort offers a safe, effective option for the majority of people with depression.[1] This includes people with seasonal affective disorder (SAD, or "winter blues"), too.[2] But not everyone with depression should use it. Some people respond only to certain types of antidepressants. Severe or treatment-resistant depression is also best treated with standard drugs.

Clinical experience shows that people who are unable to tolerate conventional antidepressant drugs, like Elaine, do well with it. Its very low number of side effects means that even the most sensitive people usually have no problems in taking it. In fact, as studies have proven, the vast majority of people who use St. John's wort experience no side effects at all.[3]

This is also great news for older people, since they're especially vulnerable to the side effects of conventional drugs. As we grow older, our bodies become less able to compensate for the adverse effects of medications. Actually, it's no exaggeration to say that the side effects of the drugs are one of the biggest causes of illness and hospitalization in the elderly today. We desperately need safer alternatives.

That's why American geriatricians—doctors who specialize in treating old people—are sitting up and taking notice of St. John's wort. An entire issue of the *Journal of Geriatric Psychiatry and Neurology,* for instance, was recently devoted to articles about it. In an editorial, Dr. Michael Jenike, professor of psychiatry at Harvard Medical School and the Massachusetts General Hospital, described St. John's wort as "very exciting," and "a particularly attractive choice for treating mild-to-moderate depressions in our elderly patients."[4]

St. John's wort is also especially useful for depressed people who have a lot of physical symptoms, like chronic fatigue, or recurrent infections. That's because it's not just an antidepressant. It actually has powerful effects on the immune system as well as the brain. Studies show it works to correct imbalances in immune functioning, helping people feel better physically as well as emotionally.[5]

St. John's wort is also helpful in the treatment of anxiety.[6] It provides a feeling of calmness and decreases the effects of stress on the body and mind. Unlike conventional drugs used to treat anxiety, it doesn't cause drowsiness or difficulty in concentrating, so it's safe to take when you're driving.[7] It's also nonaddictive, which is another big advantage.

Like Prozac, St. John's wort can help people who feel oversensitive to social rejection. It doesn't numb their ability to feel emotions, however, as many drugs used in psychiatry do. Instead, St. John's wort helps by protecting against the big drop in mood that occurs when people feel rejected by others or are otherwise upset. Many patients report that it acts like an emotional anchor for them, so that they are not swept away in the currents of their negative emotions. As a result, they are not as badly affected by difficulties in their daily life and relationships.

This is probably the main reason why drugs like Prozac are

so popular in today's world. Never before have people been subjected to so much social stress. Until this century, most people lived in communities where people all knew each other and shared a common set of values. They grew up with their neighbors, and had large, extended families nearby who could be counted on to provide support when needed. These days, our society has become increasingly fragmented. Most people live in small, nuclear families, or alone, far from their relatives and childhood friends. And we interact with more strangers in one day than people who lived two hundred years ago did in a whole year. This combination of isolation amidst the crowd is a setup for social stress and for feelings of rejection.

Because Prozac helps make people less vulnerable to this stress, it has become a kind of lifestyle accessory for many in our society. In European countries like Germany, Austria, and Denmark, where doctors are more knowledgable about herbal medications, St. John's wort fills the same need. This is not surprising, since research shows that it works in much the same way as Prozac.[8,9]

St. John's wort is good for people with insomnia, too.[10] It makes it easier for your brain to switch into its "sleep mode," so you fall asleep more quickly. In contrast to most drugs used to treat insomnia, though, it's not a sedative. Sedatives bring on sleep by shutting down your brain artificially. They cause feelings of grogginess and are often addictive. St. John's wort, on the other hand, acts in harmony with your brain's own sleep-inducing mechanism, enhancing its action instead of overriding it. As a result, your sleep is natural, and you don't have problems with grogginess or addiction. This sleep-enhancing effect takes about ten days to start to work. That's why it's best used for people with *chronic* insomnia, and not just for one or two nights.

PMS is another of the conditions for which St. John's wort is useful. This is not surprising, since many of the symptoms of PMS are similar to those of depression—restlessness, irritability, and tension, for instance. Herbalists have known about its effectiveness for premenstrual problems for hundreds of years, and today, it's still one of the most widely used natural treatments.

Why is St. John's wort useful for so many different conditions? Actually, it's not that unusual for a medication to be able to do this. Prozac, for example, is also prescribed for anxiety, insomnia, PMS, and many other things. But the healing power of St. John's wort doesn't stop at what Prozac can do—it goes well beyond it.

As you'll discover in chapter 4, St. John's wort can heal your body, too. It has a broad-spectrum antiviral effect, for one thing. It's active against the flu virus, herpes, the Epstein-Barr virus, and possibly even HIV.[11] Studies of its use in treating HIV are currently taking place at the New York University Medical Center. In addition, it has antibacterial properties, and it's effective in relieving inflammation.[12,13] Compounds extracted from St. John's wort are even being used to treat cancer in several university hospitals around the United States today.[14] Amazing!

Unlike a synthetic drug, St. John's wort contains scores of different healing compounds. There are at least ten different groups of active ingredients in it.[15] Researchers have found that no single compound in the herb accounts for all of its healing power—instead, the many different compounds work together synergistically, to produce an effect greater than any single compound could.

That's why St. John's wort is beneficial for such a wide range of the chronic health problems that are facing our society today. It is truly a healer of both the body and the mind—something that can't be said about any of our synthetic drugs.

What You Can Expect

We now have clinical data from many thousands of patients who have taken St. John's wort. As a result, we have a very clear idea of what you can expect when you take it.

First of all, like other antidepressant medications, it takes three to six weeks to take full effect. The active ingredients need to build up in your body, and your brain needs time to respond to them, producing the therapeutic effect. Taking higher doses will not speed up this process. Higher doses, however, will provide a stronger effect once the medication starts to work.

Overall, St. John's wort works as an antidepressant for around seventy percent of people who use it. This is the same percentage as for all other antidepressants. Because each person is unique in his or her biochemistry, there is no such thing as an antidepressant that is effective for everybody. If one type of antidepressant doesn't work for you, though, another type probably will. This is because they each work through slightly different biochemical pathways.

The first effect that you're likely to notice with St. John's wort is an improvement in your sleep. This usually happens by about seven to ten days after starting to use the herb. The other early effects are usually on the physical symptoms of depression—and the emotional symptoms improve afterwards. For instance, within the first few weeks St. John's wort generally improves your appetite (balancing it if it's too low or high), lessens your fatigue, and increases your general sense of physical well-being. By about the third week, it starts to lift your mood. You'll feel less depressed, and you'll also feel calmer. Many people taking it report feeling less emotionally vulnerable, as well.

These therapeutic effects are all identical to those of conventional antidepressant drugs—or even slightly better.[16,17] The biggest difference between St. John's wort and other antidepressants, however, is in the number of side effects. In a recent drug monitoring study, 3,250 patients were treated with St. John's wort. Only 2.4 percent of them reported *any* side effects.[18] This is an amazingly low number, considering that synthetic drugs like Prozac usually produce side-effect rates at least ten times higher than that.

In other words, you can expect to have no side effects from

St. John's wort. Rarely, it can cause stomach upsets, allergic reactions, or tiredness. It's important to take it in the proper dose, as described in chapter 8, since if it's taken in very high doses, it can make you sunburn easily.

There are some other basic precautions to observe in using it, as well. It's not recommended for pregnant or breastfeeding women, for instance, or for children. St. John's wort can also interact with some medications—such as other antidepressants, diet pills, and certain cold and flu medications. See chapter 6 for more information.

Apart from its low rate of side effects, you can expect to notice several other advantages of St. John's wort when you take it. For example, many people have reported that they have a higher immunity to infections when they're taking St. John's wort. When there's a flu going around at their home or work, they might be the only one who doesn't fall ill. Or they might have fewer and smaller outbreaks of herpes. Or their chronic viral fatigue might get better for the first time in months. It's only effective against certain types of viruses, though, and unfortunately, not against the viruses that cause the common cold.

Another advantage of St. John's wort is its price. Expect to pay less than half of what you'd spend on Prozac or Zoloft. The reason for this is that herbs are not patentable. That means that drug companies can't hold a monopoly on them, as they can on their synthetic drugs. Anyone can grow and sell herbal medications, keeping the prices far more competitive.

All of these benefits add up to another thing that you can

expect: St. John's wort is going to revolutionize the treatment of mild depression. It's already done this in Europe.

But in contrast to other revolutionary medications, St. John's wort is not just some new chemical drug cooked up in a test tube. In the next chapter, we'll look at how it's been a trusted part of the great healing traditions around the world for thousands of years.

Chapter 2

WHAT IS ST. JOHN'S WORT?

Presenting the Prozac of the Twenty-first Century

When we think of progress, we usually think of high-tech inventions like faster computers, or synthetic chemicals, and so on. Another kind of progress, however, is when we rediscover the value of the things that were right under our noses all along.

The story of St. John's wort is about that kind of progress. St. John's wort is a small, unimpressive-looking shrub that grows at the roadsides and in fields around the world. You have almost certainly seen it yourself, but did not recognize it. Even though the scientific world has discovered its potent medicinal power only in the last decade, it has a long and noble tradition of use by healers in many lands. We know that it has been used by herbalists in Europe, for example, for at least two thousand years. But the plant is actually far older than that.

St. John's wort, or to use its official botanical name, *Hypericum perforatum,* is a truly ancient herb. Botanists believe that the group of plants called *Hypericum* originated hundreds of millions of years before human beings evolved, when the continents of the world were still fused into a giant landmass that geologists now call Gondwanaland. Because Gondwanaland slowly broke up and drifted apart, today we find varieties of *Hypericum* spread throughout most of the continents.[1]

The most widespread variety is *Hypericum perforatum* (St. John's wort)—the one we use medicinally in the Western world. Many other varieties of hypericum are still used by traditional herbalists in places like Nepal, Siberia, and the Middle East, but they are harder to find in Europe and the United States.

St. John's wort is so widespread and hardy that it is actually one of the most common "weeds" in the world. It grows wild all over the United States and Canada, throughout Europe, the Middle East, Asia, Africa, and Australia. It prefers to grow on land that has been damaged. Recently logged forest areas, new construction sites, roadsides, or fields that have been overgrazed by cattle are some of the places you're likely to find it.

What Does It Look Like?

It's a small shrub with slender, straight stems and spade-shaped leaves that are bright green. It usually grows to a height of between one and two feet (about half a meter). Its golden yellow flowers have five petals, and they bloom only for a short time in midsummer, around the time of St. John's Day in Germany. The blossoms usually appear right on or before June 24. This day was once celebrated as a festival devoted to Balder, the Teutonic sun god. With the coming of Christianity, it was said to be John the Baptist's birthday. That's why the Germans call the plant *Johanniskraut,* or "John's plant," and why we call it St. John's wort. *Wort* is the Middle English word for "plant."

Perhaps you know this plant by one of its many other names. In the United States, it's often called Klamath weed, after the Klamath River of California, around which it grows abundantly. In the state of Washington, the locals call it goat weed, since cattle dislike it, but goats eat it. According to many authorities, St. John's wort is also none other than the legendary Rose of Sharon, mentioned in the Bible's Song of Songs.

St. John's wort is a perennial, which means that it lives for several years. Each year, after its flowers turn a rusty brown color and drop off, it produces a large number of small, tulip-shaped seed pods, each with a few tiny black seeds in it. Then the plant dies back during the winter, leaving only a short, tough little clump of stems. In the spring, it sends up new shoots again.

When the buds, flowers, or leaves of St. John's wort are crushed, a blood-red oil seeps out. This oil contains the active medicinal ingredients of the plant. According to an ancient healing tradition called the Doctrine of Signatures, plants were thought to contain clues in their physical appearance about the conditions they were beneficial for. The red oil of St. John's wort probably inspired early healers to experiment with its use for healing wounds, inflammation, and infections. These are all conditions in which part of the body turns red, because of increased blood flow.

Today we know that St. John's wort really does contain substances that help heal wounds, soothe inflammation, and fight infections, as I'll discuss in chapter 4. So the ancient herbalists were right all along. They also made another important discovery, though: that their patients who were taking it started to feel better emotionally, too. The effect seemed magical to them, as we'll see.

A Tale of Natural Magic

St. John's wort was used long before the time of the Greek and the Roman empires, but the earliest records of its use come down to us from them. They used it to treat injuries, burns, and infections, and also believed that it protected against witches' spells. By this they probably meant that it protected against states of overwhelming mental distress, such as those which we would today call depression or anxiety disorders. These states can often develop for no obvious reason, and are believed in many societies to be the result of witchcraft.

Later on, Christians continued to use St. John's wort to heal physical ailments and to protect themselves from sorcery. According to legends, Crusaders used the flowers and leaves, mashed in lard, to heal their sword wounds. There was a belief that the plant sprang up originally from John the Baptist's blood when he was beheaded, and that it contained a sort of mystical power. A poem from a manuscript dating back to 1400 declared:

> St. John's wort doth charm all witches away
> If gathered at midnight on the saint's holy day.
> Any devils and witches have no power to harm
> Those that gather the plant for a charm.[2]

The classic textbooks of European herbalists throughout the centuries hailed St. John's wort as an excellent medicine for internal and external wounds and for the treatment of melancholia (depression) and hysteria. It remained largely a folk medicine, though, its lore passing down orally from generation to generation of healers. Most of the population had no access to qualified doctors, and so they relied on the knowledge of local wise women and men. Women were most often the ones who were acquainted with the healing powers of herbs, and because of this, they were constantly in danger of being accused of being witches. It was a risky job.

Around the end of the nineteenth century, practitioners of the style of medicine we now call "conventional medicine" began to use political means to force all the other kinds of healers out of business. With refined drugs and surgery as their main healing tools, they spurned the use of herbs, which they believed were primitive, unscientific, and at best, only "pretend" drugs. Most American doctors today are the heirs to this tradition.

Alternative healers, though, continued to practice as a kind of medical underground, often with a large popular following. Naturopaths, herbalists, and others kept alive the folk wisdom about St. John's wort in the English-speaking countries of the world. They tended to prescribe it as a "women's tonic," for the relief of PMS and menstrual discomfort. Today in health food stores you still see a lot of preparations in which St. John's wort is mixed with other herbs for "women's problems." It *is* effective for PMS, but is also good for many other conditions, and is just as useful for men.

The non–English speaking Europeans have been the main ones who have continued to use St. John's wort for a wide range of problems. In Germany, for example, herbal medicine was never really forced underground in the way that it was in the United States. Instead, conventional German doctors incorporated the use of herbs into their work, and have continued to do so to this day. In German medical schools, courses in herbal medicine are part of the normal curriculum. Eighty percent of German doctors now prescribe herbs. St. John's wort has long been a registered medicine there, relied upon by family doctors, internists, neurologists, and psychiatrists. It goes by the trade names of Psychotonin M, Jarsin, Neuroplant, and a number of other brands. In 1993 alone more than 2.7 *million* prescriptions for St. John's wort extract were filled in Germany.[3]

Because of this enlightened, nonpolitical attitude about

herbs, German doctors have led the world in scientific studies of St. John's wort and many other valuable healing herbs. It is thanks to their efforts that we now know that St. John's wort is as effective as standard antidepressants for depression. With the political and financial stranglehold that conventional medicine has in the United States, those studies probably never would have been done here.

Throughout Europe, St. John's wort extract is a part of everyday life. In Denmark, for instance, a sizable percentage of the population has a sip of the alcohol-based extract every morning as they get out of bed, much as Americans have a cup of coffee. They consider it a general tonic for dealing with the stresses and strains of modern life. It is sold in beautiful glass bottles with a picture of the plant engraved on the side. St. John's wort is also used as a flavoring agent in drinks, like vermouth. The extract has a musty, raspberrylike aroma, which reminds you that it comes from a flower, and it has a rich burgundy color.

How Is It Prepared?

The St. John's wort that is used for medicine is usually *wildcrafted*. That means it is allowed to grow wild and untended, rather than being planted, watered, and weeded like most other crops. It does best if it's just allowed to do its own thing.

The flower buds contain the highest proportion of the medicinal red oil, and are the part of the plant that is harvested. The buds only appear for a brief period each year, in June.

That is why St. John's wort was traditionally "gathered . . . on the saint's holy day," as in the poem on page 32. Harvesters try to pick the buds before the flowers open. They either pull them off by hand or cut them off with scissors. The leaves and opened flowers also contain some oil, so they are sometimes taken too. The harvesters carry a bucket of alcohol or glycerine with them into the fields, so they can put the herbs straight into it before they dry. That way the precious volatile oils do not evaporate away.

The herb is then finely ground, and left to soak in the alcohol or glycerine. The oil dissolves out into the liquid, turning it a brilliant burgundy color. The inactive residue of the herb is then strained out, and the liquid extract is packaged for sale in small brown glass bottles.

Some companies sell the herb in a dried form, which is used to make tea. Others freeze-dry the buds, grind them up, and fill capsules with them.

Can I Harvest and Prepare It Myself?

Since St. John's wort grows everywhere, you might be tempted to go out and harvest some near your home. I wouldn't recommend this, though, for two reasons: First, it looks very similar to several other plants, and you might pick the wrong herb and poison yourself. Second, many farmers, highway workers, and city council crews are engaged in a campaign to eradicate St. John's wort, spraying it with herbicides like 2,4D or Roundup. The herb is so hardy, however, that these poisons usually don't kill it. So the plants you find might look normal, but actually be covered in invisible herbicide. Needless to say, 2,4D is poisonous.

If you're an expert in plant identification, however, and if it's growing on private land that you're certain hasn't been sprayed, or better yet if you've grown it yourself, you can harvest it. Fill a jar with chopped buds, top it up with vodka or vegetable oil, cover, leave it for a few days, and then strain it. Then it's ready for use.

For the rest of us, information on where to buy St. John's wort, and which forms of it are best, can be found in chapter 7.

Chapter 3

ST. JOHN'S WORT WORKS— HERE'S THE PROOF

The Truth Behind a Healing Tradition

Tradition is a great teacher, but in today's world, it's not enough. Contemporary science enjoys nothing more than to thumb its nose at tradition, to debunk old myths, and to show us that our old ways of thinking were wrong. After all, that's how we discover new things and make progress in understanding the world.

So when scientists began looking at the traditional medicine St. John's wort, they would have liked to prove that it really belonged in the mumbo-jumbo file, along with the other myths and legends. But try as they might, in one study after another, they weren't able to do that. Because this stuff really works. It doesn't just work well—it works *extremely* well.

Solid Clinical Research

There have been over thirty controlled therapy studies which have conclusively demonstrated St. John's wort's effectiveness and safety in depression.[1-13] They have included a total of several thousand patients' results, and have been published in quality medical journals. In fact, its antidepressant effects are as good as, and may even be slightly *better* than, those of imipramine, which is considered the "gold standard" in antidepressant drugs.[14]

These were not merely placebo-induced effects. These studies were double-blind and placebo-controlled, meaning that neither the doctors nor the patients knew whether they were using St. John's wort, standard antidepressants, or inactive placebos. The researchers ensured that the capsules all looked and tasted the same, and kept the identity of each of the capsules to themselves.

In 1994, for example, German psychiatrists compared imipramine to St. John's wort in a study of 135 patients with depression. They were randomly divided into two groups—one group to be treated with imipramine and the other with St. John's wort. None of the patients were told which medication they were receiving. After six weeks of treatment, the results were analyzed. As expected, the group receiving imipramine was found to be much improved. But to the psychiatrists' surprise, the group receiving St. John's wort had done even better. Seventy-five percent of them were rated as being "greatly improved" or "much improved," in contrast to only 60 percent of those on imipramine.[15]

Other studies comparing St. John's wort with standard antidepressants have shown similar results. It's been shown to be as good as or better than they are. Doctors have been astounded, and have checked and rechecked the data. In 1996, the *British Medical Journal,* one of the most prestigious journals in the profession, published an article that meticulously reexamined the data from all of these studies. The authors concluded that, indeed, "The scores on the Hamilton Depression Scale [the standard measurement scale for research on depression] after treatment were slightly better in patients on single hypericum [St. John's wort] preparations than in those on standard antidepressants." They also wrote that these "clinical trials suggest that hypericum might become an important tool for the management of depressive disorders, especially in primary care settings. . . ."[16]

As exciting as this is, however, the authors also cautioned that these are still early results. They pointed out that at present, we can confidently say that St. John's wort is better than a placebo, since studies containing several thousand patients have proven this. So far, however, the studies that specifically compared St. John's wort to standard antidepressants have only had about five hundred patients in them. Even though these studies show that it might be more effective than other drugs, the last word isn't in yet. As another recent medical reviewer wrote, it's safest to say at the present time that it "seems equally effective as standard medication."[17]

Like other antidepressants, St. John's wort is effective for between 60 and 80 percent of people who use it.[18] Also like other antidepressants, it works as powerfully as light therapy for relieving seasonal affective disorder (SAD, or "winter blues").[19]

St. John's wort's most striking effects are in improving depressed mood and difficulty in getting to sleep.[20] Researchers have also found that it has a strong ability to relieve anxiety.[21] It's also proven to help depressed people feel physically better, decreasing their headaches, fatigue, and other physical symptoms.[22]

It differs most from other antidepressants in its side effects. As studies show, it does not cause drowsiness, nor does it interact with alcohol.[23] It does not slow down reaction time, or interfere with ability to concentrate, as many antidepressants do.[24] On the contrary, there is evidence from tests of general information processing and neurological functions that it improves information processing by the brain, even in previously normal subjects—thus acting as a type of "smart drug."[25]

St. John's wort also does not interfere with the dreaming stage of sleep, as standard antidepressants do.[26] This is great news, because scientists believe that our dreams are actually essential for our well-being. Dreaming is a way for our brains to process the emotional experiences that we have during the day—it's a form of creative problem-solving in the subconscious mind.

When people are depressed, they actually dream *more,* even though they sleep less. Their dreams are intense, even exhausting. As a result, they often wake up feeling more tired than when they went to sleep. Their brains are trying very hard to solve their emotional difficulties through their dreams, in a natural, healthy response to problems.

Standard antidepressants interfere with the process of dreaming, however. Problems go unsolved, and so relapses can occur when people stop taking their medication. Unfortunately, this is a very common problem among people taking antidepressants.

St. John's wort, in contrast, allows the natural process of dreaming to continue. It works in harmony with this essential problem-solving mechanism of the brain, and not against it. So among antidepressants, it's clearly the most natural treatment choice in more ways than one.

In fact, St. John's wort is really in a class of its own in terms of how gentle it is on the body. As I mentioned in chapter 1, in the largest study to date, with more than three thousand patients, its incidence of side effects was found to be only 2.4 percent.[27] In other words, only 2.4 percent of patients reported *any* side effects, a *remarkable* figure when compared with the 30–40 percent typical of standard antidepressants. Some smaller studies have come up with different figures for side effects, ranging from zero percent *(none!)* to 20 percent,

COMPARE FOR YOURSELF!

SIDE EFFECT	PROZAC	TOFRANIL	ST. JOHN'S WORT
Nausea/vomiting	21%	18%	1%
Dry mouth	10%	56%	6%
Diarrhea	12%	12%	none
Constipation	none	27%	1%
Dizziness/Lightheadedness	6%	32%	3%
Headache	20%	24%	1%
Drowsiness	12%	32%	none
Blurred vision	none	25%	none
Racing heart	none	25%	1%
Tremor	8%	18%	none
Weight loss	13%	9%	none
Insomnia	14%	17%	none

Sources of data for table. [28-30]

but even the higher figures were only about half that of the standard antidepressants they used as comparisons.[31]

Even on those rare occasions when they do occur, the side effects of St. John's wort are usually very mild. No other antidepressant medication comes close to its level of safety.

On page 42, you'll find a table comparing St. John's wort with two of the most commonly prescribed synthetic antidepressants: Prozac and Tofranil. It shows the percentages of patients who had particular side effects from each of these medications. I've included in the table some of the *higher* estimates for the side effects of St. John's wort. Even with these high estimates, there's no contest.

How St. John's Wort Works

This remarkable herb works as an antidepressant in several different ways at once. It can do this because it contains more than ten different groups of active ingredients.[32] Fascinating evidence has emerged showing not only that St. John's wort acts on the brain, but that it boosts the immune system as well, helping to relieve the physical symptoms associated with depression. Depression is an illness that affects not only the brain, but the rest of the body, too—and St. John's wort helps by working in both these areas.

Boosting the Brain's Feel-Good Chemicals

Scientists have discovered that in people who are feeling depressed, certain changes occur in the chemistry of their brains. For example, the levels of a chemical called *serotonin* drop. Serotonin is used by the brain as a messenger, and the messages it carries are about feelings and moods. When people have a normal level of serotonin in their brain, their mood is good. But when their serotonin levels drop, they feel emotionally unstable and overly sensitive. They become irritable, anxious, and depressed. They also feel less certain of themselves in social situations, and can sometimes become more impulsive.

Prozac and St. John's wort both work by acting on the brain's serotonin system.[33,34] The fancy technical term that describes them is *serotonin-reuptake-inhibitors,* or SRIs (also known as SSRIs). In effect, these medications fool the brain into feeling that there is more serotonin around than there really is. This raises people's moods and gives them a sense of emotional stability.

So St. John's wort really is *natural* Prozac. It works in the same way. But because it contains a variety of different substances, it does much more than that. Even though the Prozac-like properties are possibly the most important way, they don't account for all of the herb's antidepressant action.

A study done in the 1980s, for instance, showed that components of St. John's wort also decreased the action of an enzyme found in the brain called *monoamine oxidase.*[35] This enzyme breaks down serotonin and other similar chemicals. Therefore, medications that decrease the action of this enzyme will *raise* the levels of serotonin in the brain, causing a mood-elevating effect. Several conventional antidepressants work this way—the *monoamine oxidase inhibitors,* or MAOIs, such as Parnate and Nardil. In many books on herbal medicine, you'll read that the reason that St. John's wort works as an antidepressant is that it is a type of MAOI.

More recent studies, however, have shown that this MAOI effect is negligible in St. John's wort in therapeutic doses, and does not account for its antidepressant effect.[36,37] The older study had erred by using unrealistically high doses. In normal doses, the Prozac-like (SRI) effect is much more important. This is actually a *good* thing, since MAOI drugs have many side effects. These include a capacity to elevate blood pressure dangerously if combined with certain foods containing the monoamine molecule tyramine, like smoked or pickled foods, wine, aged cheese, and liver. People taking MAOIs thus need to be on a restricted diet. Thankfully, this is unnecessary with St. John's wort, since its MAOI effect is negligible and no such interactions with food have ever been reported with it.

Boosting the Immune System

Aside from its effects on the chemistry of the brain, St. John's wort also has effects on the immune system, and this makes it an even more powerful antidepressant.

You might be surprised to learn that our immune systems have anything to do with our emotions. But we all know that when we become stressed-out we are more susceptible to colds and flus, and other kinds of illnesses. Scientific studies have proven that there is a very strong link between how we're feeling emotionally and how well our immune systems are functioning. The mind and the body really are one.

In depression, the immune system goes haywire. Sometimes it basically just stops working. More usually, it keeps working, but doesn't work correctly.[38] The cells of the immune system start sending out all kinds of wrong messages. For example, they send out ridiculously high amounts of chemicals called *interleukins,* which are a type of messenger for the immune system.[39] Interleukins provide a way for the cells of the immune system to communicate with each other. (*Inter-* means "between," and *leukins* means "white blood cells"—in other words, interleukins are the go-betweens for the cells of the immune system.) When too many interleukins are being produced, the cells become confused by all these messages, and they don't know what to do, just as we might feel if we were at our jobs, and suddenly received dozens of contradictory messages from our boss about what we should be working on. We'd probably be so confused that we'd be unable to do anything properly. In a similar way, when the immune system of a depressed person gets confused from too many interleukins, it becomes unable to do its job properly. The person then becomes susceptible to infections and other illnesses. That's why so many people with depression have one cold after another, or recurrent urinary tract infections, or sinusitis, and so on.

The high levels of interleukins themselves cause uncomfortable feelings in the person's body, so even if the person doesn't have an infection, they feel physically miserable. In fact, some scientists believe that the symptoms of depression—even the emotional symptoms—are all caused by too many interleukins.

This is where St. John's wort comes in. It decreases the production of interleukins. Basically, it calms down the over-activated and confused immune system, so that it starts to work properly again. Once the level of interleukins begins to fall, the symptoms of depression begin to clear up. So part of St. John's wort's antidepressant effect is due to its immune-modulating abilities.[40]

That's one reason why St. John's wort is particularly useful for depressed people who have a lot of physical symptoms or who have chronic infections. It boosts their immune systems along with their moods.

As we'll see in the next chapter, St. John's wort also has a wide range of other healing effects on physical illnesses. Quite simply, there is no other antidepressant like it.

Chapter 4

ST. JOHN'S WORT CAN HEAL YOUR BODY, TOO

Paracelsus was a famous physician of the sixteenth century, and his writings are renowned to this day. Unsatisfied with the conventional medicine he was taught at the University of Vienna, Paracelsus spent years wandering across Europe and the Middle East seeking out "old wives, gipsies, sorcerers, wandering tribes, old robbers, and such outlaws," as he wrote, to take lessons from them. He collected and recorded many of the ancient healing secrets that had previously only been passed down orally from healers to their apprentices. From his work, we've gained an insight into the otherwise unrecorded traditional uses of St. John's wort amongst the herbalists of the Old World.[1]

Thanks to his writings, we know that St. John's wort was used to treat a remarkably wide variety of conditions, ranging from skin wounds to depression to abdominal pain. And following in these traditions, herbalists today still use it for things as diverse as ear infections, PMS, and HIV.

I'd read the scientific studies about the powerful antidepressant effects of St. John's wort. I was still skeptical, though, about all these other uses. After all, in our society, we're used to drugs that have one specific purpose. We use an antibiotic for an infection, an antacid for heartburn, and so on. We have to be suspicious of things that people claim to be cure-alls, or panaceas.

But then I learned that herbs are different from the drugs we're used to. A single herb can contain hundreds of different compounds, each with different effects. Modern science has shown us that St. John's wort does indeed contain substances that help heal all of those conditions for which it was traditionally used. It really does fight infections, soothe inflammation, heal wounds, and even kill cancer cells. It's not a cure-all, of course—but it probably comes as close to being one as any other medication.

A Modern Problem, an Ancient Solution

This is the era of the virus. It's really the fault of the airplane and the passenger ship. Did you catch last winter's miserable flu virus? It came from China. Do you know someone who is HIV-positive? That virus came from Africa. In the past, viruses like these would have remained isolated in their places of origin, but because we're such a mobile species now, these exotic viruses have been able to spread all over the world.

Both the acute viral illnesses, like the flu, and chronic ones, like HIV, hepatitis C, and herpes virus infections, are more of a problem than ever.

The worst thing about viruses is that hardly any medications are effective against them. Scientists have tested countless different compounds, but only a few seem to work. One that does work is acyclovir, used against herpes infections. Another is AZT, used for HIV. And another (. . . surprise!) is *hypericin,* the main active ingredient in St. John's wort.

A Broad-Spectrum Antiviral Medication

Studies have shown hypericin from St. John's wort is powerfully active against a wide range of viruses known as lipid-enveloped viruses, including the flu virus, herpes, hepatitis C, and even HIV.[2,3] The Epstein-Barr virus, which causes mononucleosis and some cases of chronic fatigue syndrome, belongs to the herpes group of viruses, and is also included in this group. In fact, hypericin is such an exciting new antiviral treatment that researchers at the New York University Medical Center have taken out a patent on it. (Although hypericin itself can't be patented, its specific application as an antiviral treatment can be.)

Dr. Daniel Meruelo, Dr. Gad Lavie, and their associates at the NYU's department of pathology have been studying hypericin for over a decade. They've been investigating its effects on serious viral infections. "It looks like it may be a useful compound for the treatment of AIDS," said Dr. Meruelo, "especially as part of a cocktail with other drugs. There's been a trial with AIDS patients where it's shown some activity. It may be great for hepatitis C, too. And it's especially attractive in view of its low cost."

Hypericin fights viruses in two different ways: by inactivating the viruses themselves and by sitting on cell membranes and shielding them from attack by the viruses.[4] No other antiviral drug currently in use is able to do this. "We're very interested in how it works to inactivate HIV," Dr. Meruelo told me. "That's one of the main things we're trying to find out."

Dr. Meruelo is also currently studying the use of hypericin in protecting against the spread of viruses through blood transfusions.[5] "We're adding the hypericin directly to the units of blood, and we've found it completely inactivates the viruses in the blood," he said. That could be a great way to increase the safety of our blood supply. Even though the blood used for transfusions is screened carefully these days, some viruses still get through and cause infections. Hypericin could be an inexpensive way to reduce that risk.

One virus that is notorious for being spread through blood transfusions is hepatitis C. It causes a particularly nasty form of liver damage called cirrhosis, and it can lead to liver cancer. One hundred fifty thousand new cases of it are diagnosed each year in the United States alone. Unfortunately, there's no cure. In recent studies, though, hypericin has shown some promise.

Right now, at the Bronx VA Hospital and the Mount Sinai

Medical Center in New York, there's a study under way using hypericin to treat patients with chronic hepatitis C. Twenty-four patients are involved, each taking the hypericin once daily, orally. It's already been discovered through work with AIDS patients that hypericin is well tolerated in therapeutic doses, and researchers believe it has potential in a lot of different viral conditions. Later this year, for instance, a study is being planned on its use in treating warts and other viral skin problems.[6]

Skin conditions are an area of great interest to hypericin researchers. This is because one of the special qualities of hypericin is that it responds to light.[7-11] When it's exposed to light it becomes highly activated, and even more effective against viruses. So there are plans in the works to investigate it as a topical skin therapy. But we don't know if patients with deeper viral infections, like HIV, will get a better antiviral effect from it if they go out into the sun. They might. The problem is, though, that when you take high doses of hypericin, like the AIDS patients have, you become photosensitive—that is, you sunburn easily.

Interestingly, a group of researchers at Iowa State University may have come up with the solution to this problem. They've extracted a luminescent compound called *luciferase* from fireflies—the substance that makes fireflies glow—and used it to activate hypericin in the dark! They've suggested that if patients with deep viral infections are given luciferase along with hypericin, they'll have a much better antiviral effect.[12] (This prescription almost sounds like a witch's brew! *The oil of a flower and the glow of a firefly* . . .) Hypericin still works without light exposure, however, so this extra prescription is really unnecessary.

It's important to point out that all of this antiviral research has been done on refined, synthetic hypericin. It's identical to the hypericin found in St. John's wort, but it lacks all of the other medicinal compounds found in the herb. True, the unrefined St. John's wort extract, such as you can find in your health food store, has also been shown to have "impressive" antiviral activity, but we don't know if it is as effective as the synthetic hypericin.[13,14] It might be less effective, but on the other hand, it's also possible that it's *more* effective, since it contains other medicinal compounds as well as hypericin. It would be interesting to do a study comparing them.

Another thing to note is that the antiviral studies have used high doses of hypericin—from two to seven times higher than antidepressant doses. This could cause some problems. As you'll learn in the next chapter, giving a refined compound in high doses makes it more likely that you'll have side effects. Even so, apart from some photosensitivity, the researchers have found that the refined hypericin is quite safe as drugs go.

A Natural Antibiotic

Viruses aren't the only kind of bugs that St. John's wort is good for. From the days of the earliest herbalists, the mashed flowers and leaves of St. John's wort have been used to heal all manner of infections. They were used on the surface of wounds to prevent the spread of infections, and they were also taken internally, for infections in deep organs. The ancient Greek physician Pedanius Dioscorides, for instance, used it to treat "recurring fevers," by which he meant malaria. Nicolas Culpeper, an English physician of the seventeenth century, advised it be used for "spitting blood," that is, tuberculosis.[15]

We now know that St. John's wort is indeed a natural antibiotic, effective against the toughest bacteria—including the dreaded drug-resistant tuberculosis.[16] The herb contains at least two antibiotic compounds: hyperforin and novoimanine.[17,18] Unlike synthetic antibiotics, however, St. John's wort doesn't only kill bacteria. It also stimulates the person's own immune system to fight the infection, as well. For instance, it's highly active on its own against *Staphylococcus aureus*—the so-called "golden staph" bacteria, which causes serious epidemics in modern hospitals. And it also increases the immune system's ability to kill staph, in effect doubling its usefulness in treating infections.[19,20]

Candida, Shigella, and other bugs have also been successfully treated in studies with extracts of St. John's wort.[21,22] Additionally, it's effective against *E. coli,* the commonest cause of urinary tract infections. Urologists have used it as a preventive medication against such infections.[23] Because of its broad range of activities, it has also been recommended for conditions such as ear infections, sore throats, and colitis.[24]

A Healer of Wounds and a Soother of Inflammation

Across ancient Europe and Asia, St. John's wort was also a favorite remedy to speed wound healing and reduce inflammation. The Native Americans used the local species of the herb for these purposes, too. This power to heal wounds comes from the herb's combined abilities to prevent infection, stimulate the immune system, and reduce excessive inflammation and bleeding. It's an ideal treatment for battlefield injuries, and we know that it was popularly used by soldiers throughout history, up until this century.

Research by Russian scientists in 1996 has helped us to understand why St. John's wort is so effective for healing wounds. It seems that the herb contains a variety of substances that act on the immune system. Some of them stimulate immunity, and some of them suppress immunity.[25] So it's able both to *increase* the activity of a weak immune system in fighting off infections, and at the same time, to *decrease* inflammation-producing immune activity in wounds. In other words, St. John's wort tends to coax the immune response back to the harmonious middle ground. It *balances* the immune response—restoring its natural tone.

Herbalists describe plant medicines that are capable of balancing the natural tone of the body in this way as *tonics*. There are tonics for the immune system, the digestive system, the cardiovascular system, and so on.

There is no real counterpart to herbal tonics amongst the synthetic drugs. Because synthetic drugs contain only one active ingredient, they aren't capable of working in such a sophisticated, complex way as herbs can. A number of herbs act as tonics for the immune system, for instance, but no synthetic drug even comes close. This is one instance in which an herbal medicine stands head and shoulders above its synthetic counterpart. Conventional doctors could really benefit their patients by learning how to use a few herbs.

Relief from Menstrual Discomfort

One of the traditional uses for St. John's wort that is still popular today is for the relief of menstrual discomfort. It is said to be fairly effective for this, though there are no studies to back up this claim. (Note that this is quite apart from its ability to improve the symptoms of *pre*menstrual syndrome (PMS), which by definition occurs *before* the menstrual period, rather than during it.)

Menstrual cramps are believed to be caused by high levels of chemicals called *prostaglandins* in the uterus. Normally, prostaglandins regulate the menstrual flow. But when there's too much of them, they cause excessive bleeding, inflammation, and painful contractions of the muscles of the uterus. St.

John's wort probably works as a reliever of menstrual cramps by reducing the effects of prostaglandins.[26,27]

Because of its usefulness for both PMS and menstrual discomfort, St. John's wort is often recommended by herbalists as a "women's tonic." If you look in your health food store, you'll probably find it in products containing a mixture of different herbs for this purpose.

A Treatment for Cancer?

Glioma, the commonest type of brain cancer, and melanoma, a form of skin cancer, are two of the deadliest of all illnesses. Few drugs have any effect on them, and those that do are highly toxic. Very recently, studies at several institutions around the United States have shown that hypericin extracted from St. John's wort may be a safe, effective alternative.

Dr. William Couldwell is a neurosurgeon who is leading the field in this research. At the Trinity Medical Center in North Dakota, he is currently conducting a study of the effects of hypericin on gliomas, using it to treat only the most severely ill patients—people whose cancers have failed to respond to all other treatments.

"I became interested in hypericin," said Dr. Couldwell, "because it may show a similar medium of action within cells as tamoxifen." Tamoxifen is one of the most widely used modern anticancer drugs—millions of women with breast cancer, for example, take it every day. "Some patients with brain tumors have already been taking hypericin in the form of St. John's wort—it's been publicized on the Internet by brain tumor support groups. They're treating themselves, but I don't recommend or condone this."

Before Dr. Couldwell began his research, hypericin had already been shown in laboratory studies to be highly effective against cancer cells. In low doses, it stops cancers from growing, and in higher doses, especially when it's combined with light treatment, it kills the cancer cells outright, with little or no toxicity to normal cells.[28,29] But these had only been laboratory studies, using tissue cultures, or mice—no one had yet used hypericin in a *clinical* study, with human patients.

"There are about half a dozen patients enrolled in the study," said Dr. Couldwell. "The only cancer treatment they're receiving is the hypericin. They're taking it orally, in escalating doses. We're using a purified, synthetic form of hypericin, so we can be sure the effect is due to this particular component of St. John's wort, and not to any other. We're just a few months into the study right now, so it's too early to tell how effective the hypericin is. I can already say, though, that it's a very well tolerated treatment."

Dr. Couldwell's cautious optimism is shared by an increasing number of researchers. At UCLA, for example, Dr. VanderWerf and colleagues have recently experimented with hypericin for treating a number of different kinds of cancers, including melanoma. They've reported excellent results, with only "trace toxicity."[30] Another team has found that breast cancer cells also respond to hypericin.[31]

To add an even more fascinating twist to this story, it seems that extracts of St. John's wort might not only be useful for the *treatment* of cancer, but they might actually *prevent* cancer from occurring in the first place. A study published in the journal *Basic Life Sciences* in 1993 demonstrated that extracts of St. John's wort had an antimutagenic effect—that is, they prevented cellular DNA from mutating due to damage from radiation.[32] A mutation, as we know, is the first step in the development of cancer.

Numerous other herbs were tested in this study, but none of the rest had this remarkable protective effect. In another recent study, St. John's wort extract was also shown to be reliable in protecting delicate tissues such as the bone marrow and the lining of the intestines from damage due to radiation.[33]

Again, these are only laboratory studies, but they indicate that St. John's wort is indeed one of the most potentially useful medications known to science. Few other medications come close to having as broad a range of therapeutic effects, except for a handful of other herbal medications. For instance, garlic contains a natural antibiotic, and it can also reduce blood pressure and cholesterol, and prevent blood clots. Also, aspirin, which was originally extracted from the bark of the white willow tree, can relieve pain and inflammation and also prevent heart attacks and even bowel cancer. And ginseng can lower cholesterol, stimulate the immune system, and counteract fatigue. Notice that these "wonder drugs" are all either herbal or extracted from a plant. In general, herbal medications have a much broader range of uses than synthetic ones.

So why aren't they prescribed more often? Scientifically speaking, the way that most American doctors ignore herbs makes no sense at all. In the next chapter, we'll look at the reasons why most doctors are still turning a blind eye toward these valuable tools for healing.

Chapter 5

WHY DOCTORS ARE STILL STUCK ON TOXIC DRUGS

Herbs are effective and safe—it's been proven. So why do most doctors continue to ignore them? Why do they continue to prescribe toxic synthetic drugs, even though said drugs are no more effective?

Sadly, the way that doctors treat patients often has little to do with medical science. At the present time in North America and Australia, it's only the occasional clinician like myself who seems to be taking advantage of the research on St. John's wort to help their patients. The situation is different in Europe, where St. John's wort is a registered medicine, prescribed and trusted by conventional physicians.

I predict that doctors in the rest of the world will change their prescribing habits eventually—because their patients will demand it. In this age of information, news about scientific advances, such as the breakthrough studies on St. John's wort, is becoming more and more accessible to all of us. People are already learning about the many safe and effective treatments that alternative medicine offers, and they're demanding them as never before.

But why don't all doctors in the English-speaking world know about St. John's wort? A number of factors in the medical system are working against widespread acceptance of herbs. Simple ignorance and prejudice against herbal medications are two big factors. But overshadowing those, by far, are the financial and political influences exerted on the medical profession by the drug companies.

Can the Drug Companies Be Trusted?

The goal of the drug companies is basically the same as that of all other companies: making money. And boy, do they make money. The global market for antidepressants alone is estimated to be worth nearly six *billion* dollars. Thanks to extensive legislation, designed to protect consumers from unsafe new drugs, it's very expensive for these giant multinational companies to do their research and development. As a result, the companies need to get a high return on their investment in the drugs to recoup their expenses. The only way that the drug companies can get the high returns they need is to be able to patent the drugs they produce. That way, they can hold a monopoly on them and charge whatever they like for them, ensuring that they will cover their expenses and make a hefty profit to boot.

Unlike synthetic drugs, herbs are not patentable. Anyone can grow them and sell them, driving down the price and the profit margin. It doesn't make financial sense for drug companies to do research on herbs or market them. Since the overwhelming majority of research on medications is funded by drug companies, nonpatentable medications such as herbs tend to be systematically ignored.

All of this would not be so bad if doctors were not so dependent on the pharmaceutical industry. Most doctors receive most of their information about their own profession from the drug companies either directly, through advertising, seminars, freebies, and so on, or indirectly, by relying on the recommendations of academic specialists, who frequently hold positions both with drug companies and universities. This information, apart from generally ignoring safer alternatives to synthetic drugs, is often extremely biased or downright misleading.

Here is just one of many examples of this from my own experience: A young woman with depression had been started on a new antidepressant by her previous doctor. The drug had been recently introduced into Australia where I was working, but overseas doctors had already had considerable experience with it. A large, expensive-looking monograph on the drug, the size of a journal, had been distributed to doctors when the drug was introduced and claimed to give comprehensive information on the drug, including details of its side effects.

I first began to care for this patient after she had had a grand mal seizure for the first time in her life, which led to her admission to the hospital. Suspicious of the new drug, I ceased it, and looked up the chapter on side effects in the drug company monograph. In the two-page chapter, there was no mention of seizures, but plenty of reassurances about how well tolerated the drug was. Not satisfied, I went to the library to find an independent reference on the drug. It seems that in fact, in countries overseas over the last few years, there had been considerable concern over this drug's tendency to cause seizures. It had almost been taken off the market, because more people were having seizures with it than with any other kind of antidepressant. But you would never have known this if you had relied on what the drug company had told you.

Unfortunately, this story is not an isolated anomaly. This kind of thing happens all the time. Quite simply, doctors cannot trust drug companies to tell the whole truth.

Most doctors have a fatalistic attitude about side effects anyway. "There are two kinds of drugs," goes the medical saying, "drugs with side effects, and drugs that don't work." Attitudes like this are symptomatic of the general sense of therapeutic pessimism throughout conventional medicine. And of course, they ignore the fact that some medications cause frequent and severe side effects, while others are virtually free of them.

Patients, understandably, are not so blasé about these matters. Side effects are the most common cause of noncompliance with antidepressant medications (i.e., not taking as prescribed). And therefore, they're probably the most common cause of treatment failure. Even in scientific studies, where the patients and doctors are more highly motivated than in everyday practice, around five to ten percent of patients on conventional antidepressants simply quit taking them because they can't stand the side effects. In everyday practice, the percentage is probably closer to thirty or forty—but doctors don't really know for sure, because patients often won't admit to giving up the drug, for fear of "letting down" the doctor.

In contrast, because St. John's wort is so much better tolerated than other antidepressants, patients are much less likely to give it up. In a large study of patients taking St. John's wort extract for depression, only 1.45 percent of them quit because of side effects.[1]

A Game of Medical Truth . . . or Consequences

The blame for the medical profession's failure to use herbs like St. John's wort does not lie entirely with the drug companies. After all, *doctors* are the ones who write the prescriptions.

The fact is that many doctors are simply prejudiced against herbs. They think herbalists are just selling hocus-pocus and fairy tales, more akin to snake oil than medicine. True, the alternative medical industry has partly brought this prejudice on themselves. Too often, they have made claims for their products that are far beyond the scientific truth. Even today, it's difficult to separate the hype from the facts in the health food industry.

As a result, though many doctors are curious about herbal medications, there's a generalized belief in the profession that herbs are only "pretend" drugs, more likely to do harm than good.

This prejudice is further supported by the conspicuous lack of education about herbs that doctors receive in medical school. The only time herbal medications were mentioned in my medical school curriculum was when we were given warnings to look out for licorice poisoning as a cause for high blood pressure and comfrey as a cause of hepatic vein thrombosis. We were informed that many of our conventional medications, like aspirin, morphine, quinine, and digoxin, had initially been extracted from herbs, but we were also taught that this process of extraction and refinement of the effective ingredient had made the final product far superior. Refinement, we were taught, provided purer drugs, by eliminating all the myriad other "useless" compounds found in the original herb. The resultant refined product, then, was said to be more effective, more predictable in its effects, and therefore safer (theoretically).

That sounds reasonable. I accepted it as true, too—until I learned a few basic facts about herbs.

The truth is that the standard medical dogma contains some seriously mistaken ideas about herbs. Famed medical herbalist Dr. Andrew Weil discusses this in his book *Health and Healing*. "The idea that plants owe their effects to single compounds is simply untrue," he writes. "Drug plants are always complex mixtures of chemicals, all of which contribute to the effect of the whole." It is true that they do usually contain one ingredient in a higher concentration than the others. The other similar compounds that the plant contains, however, work synergistically with it to produce an overall effect greater than that which could be produced by any one ingredient alone.[2]

Opium, as an example, contains not only morphine, but also a variety of other opioids, like papaverine and codeine. Each of these has a slightly different action in the body. Papaverine, for instance, is a muscle relaxant. It provides pain relief through a different mechanism from morphine's, hence supplementing its effects.

Similarly, scientists have been unable to locate any *single* substance in St. John's wort that alone accounts for all of the plant's action. As I discussed earlier, it seems that there are a number of different substances in it that are the effective antidepressant ingredients, and that they enhance one another's actions. Researchers have therefore recommended that extracts of the whole plant be used, rather than just a single compound in it.[3]

Because a variety of synergistic healing effects are being produced, the overall dose of an herbal medication can be smaller, and less concentrated, than if you were using a single synthetic drug. This means that toxicity is much less likely to occur. Interestingly, even conventional pharmacologists (doctors who specialize in studying the use of drugs) sometimes recommend using a variety of different drugs together in low doses in patients where side effects from a single drug are a problem. But this was nature's answer all along. Nature packages lots of different healing ingredients together in low doses in one herb.

Another reason herbs are less toxic is that their active ingredients are less concentrated, and often less soluble than refined drugs, so they are more slowly absorbed. This produces steadier, lower concentrations of medicine in the system—a sort of built-in safety mechanism. Synthetic drugs are plagued by problems of toxicity due to their rapid absorption. They reach high peak levels in the bloodstream, and then rapidly fall again, making the correct dose of drug difficult to achieve. The levels seesaw back and forth between the therapeutic range and toxic range. Recently, many conventional drugs have become available in "sustained release" forms, which are more slowly absorbed, with fewer toxic peak levels. But again, this was nature's answer all along.

So, contrary to the dogma doctors are presented with during their medical educations, herbal medications are generally much safer and often as effective as refined drugs. St. John's wort is a case in point.

The Future of St. John's Wort

I believe that St. John's wort has the potential to really shake up the drug companies' monopoly on the antidepressant market. Because it's cheap, and nonpatentable, and highly effective, it could easily make Prozac and the other synthetic drugs virtually obsolete.

I also predict, though, that the drug companies are not going to give up such a big chunk of the market without a fight. What will they do to fight back? This too is predictable. They'll go back to their chemistry labs, and they'll develop a synthetic version of St. John's wort. They'll take out a patent on it, and spend lots of money on research and marketing. For the reasons I explained earlier in this chapter, the synthetic version of St. John's wort will no doubt be more toxic and more expensive. It probably won't be any more effective than the real thing, either. But since there will be so much more research available on the synthetic version, doctors will probably prescribe it rather than the real herb.

These predictions about the drug companies' coming battle against St. John's wort might sound far-fetched to you. The truth, however, is that it may have already started.

In late 1996 an article was published by a team of Canadian scientists who are already experimenting with eight different synthetic compounds derived from hypericin, to see if they have antiviral effects.[4] They modified the hypericin molecule in very minor ways, making enough of a change so that it could be patented, but not so much that it lost the medicinal effects of natural hypericin. It will probably not be long before they test one of these compounds as an antidepressant. And when it hits the market, the drug companies will no doubt promote it heavily. They'll continue to be silent about the real herb, though, since there's no money in it for them. Quite simply, this is standard operating procedure for the drug industry. Many, if not most, of the drugs that doctors use today are actually just synthetic, patentable versions of healing compounds found naturally in plants.

Fortunately, we still have access to the real thing. Herbal medications are on sale everywhere, and even though the U.S. Food and Drug Administration (FDA) may be trying to restrict your access to them, this situation isn't too likely to change in the near future.

In any case, since you have access to it, you're probably wondering whether St. John's wort is right for you. In the next chapter, you'll find some more important points to consider in making that decision.

Chapter 6

IS ST. JOHN'S WORT FOR YOU?

Each and every one of us is unique, on every level of our beings—from the way we think to the biochemical reactions going on in our cells. As a result, a medicine that is good for one person may not be good for another. So far you've read about how St. John's wort has helped other people. Maybe you're wondering if it's right for you. In this chapter, we'll look at how to make that decision, and we'll go through some basic points for using St. John's wort safely.

Two Important Points

How do you start to take St. John's wort? There are two very important points that I want to make here. First of all: *Take St. John's wort only with the cooperation of your doctor.* The care of a doctor is vital not only for diagnosis and prescribing treatment, but for monitoring the effects of treatment. He or she should be involved with your decisions to use any medicine, for your sake, in the unlikely event that anything untoward does happen, such as an unusual side effect. And as mentioned above, St. John's wort is not for everybody—you might need a different approach to treatment.

Second: *If you have any symptoms of depression, you need to see a doctor immediately.* Depression can be a very serious illness. It's crucial that you get professional assistance to meet your unique needs. No book could ever replace the healing power of a therapeutic relationship. By all means, if you're feeling overwhelmed or suicidal, reach out and get the help you need without delay.

Are You Depressed?

What is depression? As I mentioned in the introduction, it's one of the commonest of all illnesses—almost everybody will experience its symptoms at some time in their lives. Around fifteen percent of people, though, will have them to such a severe degree that doctors would say they have *major depressive disorder.* According to the current bible of psychiatrists around the world, the fourth edition of the *Diagnostic and Statistical Manual of Mental Disorders* of the American Psychiatric Association, a person has to have certain symptoms to be diagnosed with major depressive disorder. You'll find them in the table on page 73. In real life, however, things come in shades and degrees. A person may not necessarily meet the classic criteria for depression. It's important to trust your own instincts about how you're feeling as well as to gain feedback from an outside source.

CRITERIA FOR MAJOR DEPRESSIVE DISORDER

Five or more of the following symptoms over a two-week period, occurring daily or nearly every day (and one of the symptoms must be either [1] depressed mood, or [2] loss of interest or pleasure in life):

1. Depressed mood for most of the day
2. Loss of interest or pleasure in life
3. Change in appetite, or weight loss of more than five percent of body weight
4. Insomnia or excessive sleep
5. Acting or feeling either agitated or slowed down
6. Fatigue or loss of energy
7. Feelings of worthlessness or excessive, inappropriate guilt
8. Poor concentration or indecisiveness
9. Recurrent thoughts of death or suicide, or a suicide plan or attempt

Table adapted from DSM-IV, *Diagnostic and Statistical Manual of Mental Disorders,* ed 4. (Washington, D.C.: American Psychiatric Association, 1994).

You might be surprised to learn that in many cases, people with depression do not really know that they have it. This is because it can produce so many different symptoms. Having seen hundreds of patients with depression, I've been struck by the individual differences in their experiences. One young man I treated, for example, presented with the main symptom of memory loss. A middle-aged woman's primary symptom was anxiety. A young woman had feelings of irritability and anger, and she felt they were out of control. Another young man described consuming self-doubts and a complete inability to sleep. A middle-aged man felt that the world was empty and purposeless. Another middle-aged woman came to me with complaints of pain throughout her body. Yet there was no doubt that all of these people were suffering from major depressive disorder.

It has been said that depression tends to exaggerate a person's character traits. A person who is a worrier will worry more, an angry person will become angrier, and a poor sleeper will become sleepless. Although we all have many things in common, each person is like a world in themselves, and each requires individual assessment and therapy to meet his or her unique needs.

Where to Start

To meet your unique needs, the best person to go to first is your local family doctor. He or she will know what to look for to diagnose your problem accurately (sometimes this is very difficult, even for experts on depression). Your doctor will also be able to look for medical conditions that might be causing your depression and will help work out what sort of therapy might be best for you. He or she might refer you to a psychologist or a psychiatrist.

There are times when psychiatric help can be lifesaving. People whose depression is severe or is not responding to basic therapies should see a psychiatrist, who has much more experience in treating severe depression than a family doctor or an alternative therapist. Suicidal ideas are a clear indication that help should be sought straightaway, from the local hospital's emergency room if necessary. A short stay in a hospital can give people enough "time out" from their difficulties to break the cycle of depression and approach the situation anew.

However, the majority of people with depression are only mildly depressed and are treated by family doctors. This is the way it should be. Family doctors are the ones who know their patients best and who can most easily be reached if there's a problem.

Getting the Best Medication for You

In spite of the above recommendations for seeing family doctors, if you go to a conventional doctor for help with depression, no matter how mild your symptoms are, no matter how long they've been present, and no matter what the cause is, you are almost guaranteed to be prescribed a synthetic antidepressant drug. This may or may not be the best thing for you.

I am not ideologically opposed to the use of synthetic anti-depressant medications. I prefer to avoid getting caught up in ideologies and dogmas, and instead judge treatments by their actual ability to help people get better. Antidepressant drugs do work; they are successful in relieving depression in about sixty to eighty percent of people who use them. They are often indispensable in the treatment of severe depression; they have probably saved hundreds of thousands of lives. I prescribe them frequently, for patients with treatment-resistant or otherwise severe cases of depression. On the other hand, I prefer to use St. John's wort for the treatment of *mild* depression, since it is a superior medication overall for that purpose.

How can you make sure that you're being prescribed the best treatment for your particular circumstances? Talk to your doctor. Tell him or her that you've read about St. John's wort and would like to try it. If your doctor hasn't caught up with the research on it, show him or her this book or a photocopy of appendix 4: "For the Health Professional: Review Articles on St. John's Wort." This appendix provides references for recent journal articles that review, critique, and summarize the dozens of published clinical studies on the use of St. John's wort to treat depression.

Once your doctor knows about St. John's wort, he or she will probably be willing to prescribe it. If he's not, ask him why. Don't assume he is close-minded. He may have good reasons why he does not want to prescribe it for you. It's not suitable for everyone. For example, if your depression is anything more than mild, I'd recommend you use another medication.

In spite of my criticisms of doctors in the last chapter, most doctors I know are very open-minded, reasonable people. They will generally accept a treatment that has been demonstrated to work in proper scientific trials. After all, they do want the best for their patients. With St. John's wort's remarkable track record, doctors will soon come to know about and prescribe it.

When You Should Not Use St. John's Wort

In quite a few situations, St. John's wort should definitely *not* be used, and it's important for you to know about them.

Pregnant women should not take St. John's wort. Taking any medicine carries a risk of birth defects. True, none have been reported with St. John's wort, but studies haven't been done on this issue yet. So we need to play it safe. Likewise, if you're a woman in your childbearing years and are not using adequate contraception, you should not use this herb.

In addition, nursing women and children under 12 should not use St. John's wort. No studies have been done on the use of this herb in babies or young children. Their metabolisms are different from those of adults, and until we know more, it should not be given to them.

People with liver or kidney diseases should only receive St. John's wort (or any medication) under close medical supervision. The liver and kidneys are the body's disposal system, and if they're not working, medicines can easily build up in the body to reach toxic levels. People with heart failure should also avoid St. John's wort.

If you have high blood pressure, you should discuss this with your doctor. Some books on herbal medicine recommend avoiding St. John's wort in this circumstance. The reason for this is that a study in the 1980s suggested that this herb works in a similar way to monoamine oxidase inhibitors (MAOIs), which are known to cause problems with blood pressure. As I discussed in chapter 3, when a person taking a MAOI drug eats foods that contain the amino acid tyramine, blood pressure can go dangerously high—especially if the patient already has high blood pressure. People on these drugs therefore need to avoid foods with tyramine in them. Herbalists worried that St. John's wort might share this problem.

Studies in the 1990s, however, have shown that the MAOI-like effect of St. John's wort is negligible when it's used in normal doses. So it is very unlikely that it would react with tyramine. In fact, no such reactions have been reported with it. In Germany, where doctors have had the most experience with St. John's wort, it is considered safe to use in patients with high blood pressure.

Nonetheless, if you have high blood pressure, and your doctor agrees to your use of St. John's wort, I recommend the following additional precautions be taken: (1) Have your blood pressure checked at least weekly for the first six weeks, and at least monthly thereafter. (2) Do not eat foods contain-

DO NOT USE ST. JOHN'S WORT IF YOU ARE TAKING ANY OF THE FOLLOWING:

DRUGS/SUPPLEMENTS	COMMENTS
Antidepressants of any kind.	See page 80 for details.
Other medications for mental illnesses, such as antipsychotics (e.g., haloperidol, chlorpromazine, clozapine, etc.) and lithium.	St. John's wort does not work for bipolar disorder (manic depression). Like other antidepressants, it may even make mania worse. It also doesn't work for schizophrenia. It can interact with drugs used for its treatment, as well.
Diet pills, nasal decongestants (including cold and flu mixtures), or medications for hay fever or asthma.	These drugs often contain mono-amines, which can possibly interact with St. John's wort, causing high blood pressure and other problems. Certain asthma medications, though, such as cromolyn sodium and steroid inhalers, are fine to take with St. John's wort—check with your doctor first.
Illicit drugs, or narcotics (such as cocaine, amphetamines, or meperidine).	These may also interact dangerously with St. John's wort. In addition, you should be aware that narcotics and most kinds of illegal drugs can actually cause depression.

DRUGS / SUPPLEMENTS	COMMENTS
Amino acid supplements, including phenylalanine and tyrosine.	Amino acids are a form of monoamines, which, as mentioned above, can pose a danger when mixed with St. John's wort. The monoamines that you get in your diet (e.g., amino acids in meat), are less concentrated and are not a hazard, however.

ing tyramine. They are: alcohol (especially beers and wines); fava beans (broad beans); all cheeses except cream cheese and cottage cheese; liver; pickled or smoked meats, fish, or poultry; packaged soups; orange pulp; yeast and meat extracts (e.g., Marmite and Bovril); and sausage. In addition, have no more than one or two servings a day of the following foods: soy sauce, sour cream, yogurt, bananas, avocados, eggplant, plums, raisins, spinach, and tomatoes.

Many other medications and even some nutritional supplements can potentially interact with St. John's wort, and should not be taken with it. They include all other kinds of antidepressants—this is an important point, since you may already be taking one. If you are, you need to talk to your doctor. If they agree to give St. John's wort a try for you, your other antidepressant should be ceased *under medical supervision,* and be allowed to fully "wash out" of your system, before you start taking the herb. Above, you'll find a table of the medications that shouldn't be taken with St. John's wort.

Now that I've discussed the contraindications for using St. John's wort, I want to add one more thing. There has never actually been a report of any patient with any of the above conditions, or who was taking any of the above medicines, who had a problem with St. John's wort. The above guidelines are based entirely on theoretical grounds. They are a list of conditions where St. John's wort could quite *possibly* pose a problem.

Still, if you have any of those conditions, or are on any of those medications, I very strongly advise you not to take St. John's wort. You do not want to be the first one to have a bad reaction to it. Play it safe.

Why Medication Isn't Enough

So far we've looked at the question of how to get the medication that is the best for your particular circumstances. But medication is really only one part of a good overall treatment plan for depression. Used alone, it's inadequate. This goes for St. John's wort, too.

Most conventional doctors treat depression with medication alone, as though it were only a biochemical problem. True, biochemical abnormalities may be found in depressed people, but they are only part of the story. Depression is a process involving the mind, body, and spirit, and it needs to be taken seriously and treated on all of these levels if the illness is really to be cured. If you only treat the biochemical abnormalities, you are ignoring a large part of the person's illness.

The simple fact is that medication doesn't fix the causes of depression. That is why so many people have a relapse when they stop their medication. Their depression was really still there, all along—it's just that the symptoms were suppressed by the drug.

But depression can be cured. Its causes can be fixed. For example, depression is sometimes caused partly by negative belief systems that people have learned from their childhood. A special form of therapy called *cognitive therapy* helps people to learn more realistic ways of thinking about themselves and their lives. Cognitive therapy can cure depression. It uses no drugs, only simple exercises in speaking and thinking. Studies show it works better than drugs and that people who use it are much less likely to have relapses of depression.[1] Most doctors do not know this, and do not refer their patients to get cognitive therapy when they should.

Psychologists are the main practitioners of cognitive therapy. If you're depressed, I recommend that you ask your doctor for a referral to such a practitioner, even if you're already taking medication.

Many other psychological and physical causes of depression can also be fixed. Medical illnesses, difficult life circumstances, longstanding psychological issues, alcohol and drug abuse, erratic lifestyles, vitamin deficiencies, and many other factors that lead to depression can be changed.

That's why a holistic approach to treatment is so much more effective. Holistic medicine is about more than just biochemistry, and it uses more than just medication. It takes into account all of the other aspects of a person's life, and treats the person as a whole being—mind, body, and spirit together. Holistic medical practitioners are qualified in conventional medicine, but choose to work within this larger framework of understanding human beings.

When it comes to diagnosis and treatment, they consider much more than just a person's symptoms. They look carefully at all parts of the person's world in order to understand what the symptoms mean in the context of that person's life. They would consider the person's diet, exercise, relaxation, and work habits, for instance. They would understand that many of the things going on in a person's social, mental, and spiritual life have a great influence on how the person is feeling. People's relationships with their families, for example, are very important. So are their goals in life, what they believe in, and if they're living the kind of life they really want. In other words, holistic doctors take into account the many important ways that a person's mind and spirit affect their body, and vice versa.

To treat people on all these levels, holistic physicians employ a variety of techniques, including nutritional medicine, herbalism, acupuncture, counseling, meditation, homeopathy, physical manipulation, and many other alternative therapies, in addition to the tools of conventional medicine.

Most holistic practitioners believe that the person's own innate healing mechanisms should be supported and enhanced, rather than overridden with drugs and surgery. If conventional medication or surgery is really necessary, though, they will use them. In short, they offer the only truly comprehensive medical care available. To locate a medical doctor in your area who practices according to the principles of holistic medicine, refer to appendix 3.

I've found in my work that when depressed people are treated holistically, and the underlying causes of their illness are dealt with, they can really blossom as never before in their lives. In many cases, it's almost as though their depression was a kind of messenger to them, telling them that something in their life needed to be transformed—either within them, or in their lifestyle, or both.

A discussion of all of these underlying causes is really beyond the scope of this book. A doctor with a comprehensive, holistic approach to the treatment of depression can help you find your own personalized healing path.

Chapter 7

HOW TO BUY ST. JOHN'S WORT

Where to Buy It

Most health food stores carry St. John's wort. You might have to ask for *Hypericum,* since this is its botanical name. If it's not in stock, the proprietor will usually be happy to order it for you. It's also available through many naturopaths and other natural healers, so you could try looking these up in your phone directory if you do not live near a health food store. You can also order it from many companies through the mail, over the phone, or by fax. In appendix 1, you'll find a list of some of these suppliers and how to contact them.

If you're lucky enough to live in Germany, you can get St. John's wort directly from your regular family doctor. It's a registered medicine there, and has long been prescribed by conventional physicians. It comes in gel capsules, under the trade names of Psychotonin M, Sedariston, Jarsin, Neuroplant, and others.

Tablets, Capsules, Raw Dried Herb, or Liquid Extracts—Which Is Best?

As a general rule with herbs, the best way to purchase them is in the form of the liquid extract. This is the way St. John's wort is usually sold. The problem with raw, dried herbs and with tablets is that the exposure to air and light that they receive causes their active ingredients to break down. As a result, their potency is less reliable. Liquid extracts preserve the active ingredients best.

Herbal extracts are made by soaking crushed herbs in alcohol or glycerine, allowing the oily active ingredients to dissolve out into the liquid. The inactive residue of the herbs is then strained out. (Alcohol-based extracts are also known as *tinctures.*)

The extracts are usually sold in small brown glass bottles, with a medicine dropper that screws into the top. The dark glass protects against light-induced degradation. It's best to store them in the refrigerator to protect against heat-induced degradation, too.

Should I Buy Flower, Bud, or Leaf Extracts of St. John's Wort?

If you compare brands of extracts, you'll notice that some say that they're prepared using only the unopened flowering tops of the plants, or the buds. If it doesn't say this on the bottle, the extract was probably prepared using the leaves as well as the buds, which is more economical for the producer. Which should you buy? The short answer is that bud extracts are *probably* better.

As with a certain recreationally used herb (marijuana), the buds of St. John's wort contain the highest concentrations of the active ingredients. As a result, extracts from them are likely to be more potent. Most traditional herbalists throughout history have preferred to use the buds. I think tradition is a valuable teacher.

This is not to say that leaf extracts are no good—on the contrary, they too contain the active ingredients. Actually, some herbalists prefer to use extracts taken from the whole plant—buds, leaves, stems, and roots. They reason that different parts of the plant contain slightly different healing substances, and so extracts of the whole plant will contain the widest variety of these substances. This makes sense. Scientists do not know for certain which of the substances in St. John's wort are the active ones. It's likely, though, that the active substances are found throughout the plant. The buds contain them, and so do the leaves.

The facts are that the studies on hypericum's effect as an antidepressant haven't differentiated between the effects of the buds and the effects of the leaves. Leaf extracts should be fine to use. But if bud extracts are just as easily available, I would prefer them.

Is Organic Better?

Yes, it really is. Organically grown herbs are hardier and contain higher concentrations of nutrients and active ingredients. And of course, organic herbs are not covered in synthetic poisons that will end up in your body.

Some brands of extract are certified to be organic. Certification is important because it provides a system of verification of organic status. Otherwise, any grower could claim to be organic while spraying pesticides all they want. To be certified as organic, farms have to pass strict inspections on a regular basis.

What Does Wildcrafted Mean?

Several brands of extract state on the labels that their herbs are *wildcrafted*. This means that the herbs are allowed to grow wild rather than being cultivated. St. John's wort grows best without being tended, anyway.

How Much Does It Cost?

St. John's wort extract is made by numerous companies around the world. In appendix 1 you'll find a list of some of them and where to contact them, including sections for the United States, Canada, the United Kingdom, Europe, and Australia. Prices vary, but in the United States, all the brands of extract listed retail for between eight and ten dollars for a bottle containing one fluid ounce (30 ml.) This represents a quantity sufficient to last between one and two weeks, depending on the dose you need. For tips on finding the right dose for you, read chapter 8.

For a person using an average dose of a liquid extract, St. John's wort will cost around twenty-five to thirty dollars a month. Unfortunately, most insurance companies will not cover this cost. Then again, some insurance companies will not cover Prozac, either. Prozac costs around seventy dollars a month, even at a discount pharmacy.

Are Mixtures of Herbs Better?

St. John's wort is often sold in mixtures with other herbs. I do not recommend that you buy these. There are three good reasons for this. Let me introduce them for you with a parable from the ancient Chinese text *The Sayings of Confucius.*

The great sage Confucius once fell ill. A healer brought him a medicinal concoction made of many ingredients. Confucius thanked him, but responded, "Because I do not know this medicine, I will not take it." Sensible guy. Confucius probably knew that mixtures of medicines have a number of drawbacks.

First, if you have an adverse reaction to the mixture, it will be impossible to know which of the herbs in it was responsible. Second, using herbs one at a time is the only way to gauge their individual effectiveness for you. And third, I agree with Confucius that it's important for a consumer to know all there is to know about the medicines they're taking. Some mixtures contain so many herbs that it's difficult to know all about them and about their possible interactions with one another. Unless you are an expert herbalist, I would avoid them.

Chapter 8

HOW TO USE ST. JOHN'S WORT

In this chapter you'll get the basic, nuts-and-bolts information that will enable you to take St. John's wort safely and effectively. You'll learn about how much to take and how often. And just as important, you'll also learn about how long a period to use it for.

How Much Should I Take?

In the scientific studies of St. John's wort as an antidepressant, the dose of the extract that the patients used was standardized. The amount they took was either 3 ml or 4.5 ml per day. This translates to a total of around three fourths of a teaspoon per day (one teaspoon equals 5 ml). They divided this daily dose into three parts, so, in other words, they took one fourth of a teaspoon three times a day. You can use this as a general guideline. The extract is taken mixed into a glass of water or juice.

The dose of extract that you will need, however, depends on two other factors: the brand you are using and your age.

Some brands of extracts are more concentrated than others, and so you'll need to take less of them. The labels will tell you. They will also give you specific instructions on how many drops to use, and how many times a day.

The label will usually give a wide range of suggested doses. One brand says: "Two to five times a day take 30 to 40 drops in a little water." This means they recommend a total between 60 and 200 drops per day (about one half to one and a half teaspoons daily), which is a wide range of variation. The vagueness of their advice might be a little annoying to us, but the fact is since that only they really know how strong their extract is, we should follow their advice. I can only suggest that you start with a dose in the low to middle range of what they recommend. If you're over age 65, however, you should take less, and I've included some special recommendations for you below.

Most labels also contain the words "Fresh herb: Menstruum ratio 1:1.5," or "Fresh herb strength 1:1," or something similar. This little bit of herbal technicalese is basically a statement about how strong the extract is. The ratio refers to how much of the ground-up fresh herb went into how much of the alcohol or glycerine used in the extract.

At present, not all manufacturers in the United States standardize their extracts or tablets—in other words, the amount of active ingredients in their products varies from batch to batch. This means that the dose that you get in each drop of extract, or each tablet, is not exactly the same. This is not really a big deal, though. Because herbs like St. John's wort are so much less toxic than synthetic drugs, you have a far greater margin of safety with the dose.

In Europe, however, standardization of doses is more widely used. I've spoken to herbal manufacturers in the United States, and they say they are all probably going to go that way eventually. Many other herbal products are already standardized here, such as ginseng extracts.

How Often Should I Take It?

Even though virtually all the manufacturers say you should take it three times a day, and all the studies were conducted with thrice-daily dosing, it's probably not really necessary to do this. I do recommend you take it at least twice daily when you're starting out, however—see below.

Many people who've used St. John's wort for a long time take it only once a day. To do this, you would add up all three of the little doses that you would normally take in one day, and take them at one time, in the morning. For instance, if your normal divided dose was 20 drops three times a day, your new once-a-day dose would be 60 drops.

The reason why this is okay is that the main medicinal ingredients in St. John's wort stay active in the body for quite a long time after they're swallowed—for more than a day. This is pretty unusual for a medication. Most other medications are deactivated and excreted within a few hours, so you need to take several doses a day to make sure there's always some in your body. But since a dose of St. John's wort keeps working for more than a day, there's no real need to take the extract more than once daily.

This is great news, since it really simplifies things. It also means that it's okay if you forget to take the extract for a day or so. You'll still have enough in your body from the day before to get a therapeutic effect.

For the technically minded, the term that describes how long a substance stays in your body is called the *elimination half-life*. One half-life is the length of time that it takes to clear half of the dose of the substance out of your body. The half-life of hypericin, which is one of the most important ingredients in St. John's wort, is forty-three hours. The half-life of pseudohypericin, another important ingredient, is twenty-five hours.[1]

In spite of all this, during the first few months that you use St. John's wort, I still recommend that you take it at least *twice* a day. There are two reasons for this advice: First, there are many active antidepressant compounds in St. John's wort, and scientists haven't yet identified all of them. Although hypericin and pseudohypericin are thought to be the most important ones, there are almost certainly some others that we don't know about yet and that may have shorter half-lives. In the first few months of treatment, it's especially important to get all of the available therapeutic effect from St. John's wort. To cover all your bases, and take into account any unidentified compounds, it makes sense to take it more frequently than once a day. The second reason is that if it is taken in smaller doses, the extract is less likely to irritate your stomach.

Tablets or Capsules?

As I mentioned in the last chapter, I recommend you use extracts in preference to tablets or capsules. If you do want to use capsules, however, be aware that not all brands of tablets and capsules of St. John's wort are standardized for their hypericin content. As a result, different brands have different potencies, and you need to follow the directions on the label to know the dose to take.

In some of the studies on depression, capsules containing extract were used. The investigators weighed these out, and the dose of extract they used was usually 900 mg daily.

They used extract that was standardized to contain a certain percentage of hypericin, so that a total dose of hypericin of about 1 mg daily was given in most trials. The range of daily doses varied from 0.4 mg to 2.7 mg. I'd recommend you use the median dose, about 1 mg a day.

To give an example of how to take 1 mg daily, one brand of capsules popular in the United States contains 300 mg of the the raw herb, and is standardized to contain 0.3 percent hypericin. This would mean that each capsule contains roughly 1 mg (300 mg × 0.3%) of hypericin, so you'd only need to take one capsule per day. This can work out to be considerably cheaper than using the extract.

If You're Over 65

If you are over age 65, you should take a smaller dose, whether you use the liquid extract, tablets, or dried herb forms. I recommend that you start with the lowest dose that is suggested on the label. For instance, in the example I discussed earlier, where the suggested dose was between 60 and 200 drops per day, you would take 60. Take this low dose for four weeks or so. Increase the dose only if you haven't had an adequate effect by that time.

If the label doesn't suggest a range of doses, but instead only gives one dose for all, you should take half of this dose. For example, if the label says, "Take 30 drops three times a day," you should take 15 drops three times a day.

Do I Take It with Meals, or on an Empty Stomach?

Take St. John's wort with meals. Some manufacturers recommend taking it on an empty stomach, but there is really no good reason for this advice. One of the main reasons that so many people experience nausea and stomach upset as a side effect of medicines and vitamins is that they take them on an empty stomach. That means that the stomach lining is exposed to high concentrations of the stuff they're taking, and so it gets irritated. There are a few medications that really do need to be taken on an empty stomach, because they get inactivated by food. St. John's wort isn't one of them, though.

It's also easier to remember to take your medicine when you have it with each meal.

How to Make St. John's Wort Tea

Tea is made using the dried herb form of St. John's wort. As I mentioned in the last chapter, I don't recommend using the dried herb form. The active ingredients in the plant simply evaporate, and as a result, it's less potent. If you decide to use the dried herb, however, here is how it is done: Add one or two teaspoons of the dried herb to a cup of boiling water, and let it steep, covered, for fifteen minutes. Drink two or three of these cups per day, sweetened with honey if you wish. It's helpful to purchase a small teapot with a two- or three-cup capacity, such as the Chinese use to serve green tea. They are available for a few dollars at Chinese food stores around the world. With such a teapot, you need only make one batch per day.

How Long Does It Take to Work?

It takes St. John's wort about four weeks to work. You should start to notice some effects, though, by the tenth day. See chapter 1 for more details. If you feel better in the first few days after taking the extract, this is likely to be a placebo effect.

How Long Should I Take It For?

This question does not have a simple, one-size-fits-all answer. In general, psychiatrists recommend that people with depression take their antidepressant drug for at least six months continuously, to avoid a relapse. But some people will need to take it for a longer period.

I don't recommend that you take St. John's wort for longer than a year or so. One reason for this is that at the present time, there are no long-term studies to tell us if there are any side effects that only show up after prolonged treatment. It's true that St. John's wort has been used safely for thousands of years, and that there are many people around the world today who have been using it for decades with no problems. Chances are that St. John's wort is far safer for long-term use than any other antidepressant medication. Still, I prefer to err on the side of caution, so until long-term studies are available, it's best to play it safe and keep its use to less than a year.

When you discontinue it, do so gradually, cutting down the dose bit by bit over a period of a month or so. (Of course, if you're discontinuing it because of a side effect, you can do so immediately, without tapering it off.)

Actually, unless a person has severe, recurrent depression, I don't recommend using any antidepressant for years at a time. In our society, there are huge numbers of people who have been taking synthetic antidepressants for their whole lives. This is not a good situation at all. They are at high risk for side effects—side effects that can become more and more serious as people get older.

The main way people end up on antidepressants for life is when they do not receive any other treatment for their depression apart from drugs. Unfortunately, this is a mistake that the majority of conventional doctors and psychiatrists make all the time. As I discussed in chapter 6, medications cannot actually *cure* depression—all they do is relieve the symptoms. This includes St. John's wort, by the way. Ideally, St. John's wort, or any medication, for that matter, should be just one part of a comprehensive, holistic approach.

Chapter 9

THE SIDE EFFECTS— THEY'RE RARE, BUT THEY DO OCCUR

This chapter contains essential information for anyone who is using St. John's wort. I'm a firm believer in the principle that people should know all that there is to know about the products they buy and use, especially medications. It's bad enough experiencing side effects, but it's worse when you haven't been informed about what to expect. Doctors should talk about side effects because many of them are preventable with a few commonsense measures, as I'll explain.

The most remarkable thing about the side effects of St. John's wort is how rare they are. As I mentioned before, a 1994 drug monitering study, in which 3,250 people were treated with St. John's wort extract, found that only 79 of them reported *any* undesired drug effects. That's just 2.4 percent of them.[1]

Some smaller studies of St. John's wort have reported different rates. One recent study of 97 patients, for example, found absolutely *no* side effects from it.[2] And another study of

105 patients also reported "no notable side effects."[3] A few small studies have reported higher rates, however, up to 20 percent, but this was still only about half or less of the number of the side effects reported for the standard antidepressants they used as a comparison.[4,5] In these studies, the side effects of St. John's wort were not only much fewer in number, but were also rated by the patients as being less severe in intensity than those of the synthetic drugs.

In other words, even when they do occur, the side effects of St. John's wort are usually mild. The commonest ones are stomach and intestinal symptoms, fatigue, and skin rashes and itching. I'll discuss these effects, and the steps you can take to deal with them. There are also a number of less common side effects, which I will also discuss. If a severe side effect occurs while you are using St. John's wort, you should, of course, immediately stop taking it. If the side effect is mild, however, you may choose to continue using the herb, after consulting with your doctor.

I want to make this point clear: If any side effect occurs when you're taking St. John's wort, no matter what it is, tell your doctor about it as soon as possible. It's very important that your doctor know about it, even if it doesn't seem important to you. Thousands of years of use and, now, scientific studies have proved it to be quite safe—but everyone's biochemistry is unique. We always need to be alert when it comes to medications.

Side Effect 1: Stomach and Intestinal Symptoms

This means things like nausea (feeling as if you want to vomit), abdominal pains, loss of appetite, and diarrhea. In the large drug monitoring study I mentioned above, these symptoms were reported to occur in about 0.5 percent of patients—that's 1 in 200. It was noted that some patients actually had these symptoms before they were started on St. John's wort, so the herb may not have been responsible for these effects. Loss of appetite, nausea, and bowel upsets are common in people who are stressed-out or depressed, even when they're not on any medication.

PREVENTING STOMACH UPSETS

There are nine simple things that you can do to prevent stomach and intestinal symptoms from St. John's wort, or to decrease them if you have them:

1. Take your St. John's wort extract with meals, and not on an empty stomach. As I explained in the last chapter, taking it with food means your stomach lining will not be exposed to high concentrations of the extract, and so will not be as irritated by it. It's the irritation of your stomach lining that makes you feel nauseated and can cause your bowels to churn around uncomfortably.

2. Dilute the extract in a large glass of juice or water. This will further decrease its concentration in your stomach.

3. Instead of taking your extract one to three times a day, try

spreading it out to five times a day. Take the same total dose each day, but in smaller portions. Have three small portions with your three meals, and have two snacks in between meals when you have the other two small portions.

4. Try putting your daily extract into a 1.5-liter bottle of spring water in the morning, and sipping from it throughout the day.

5. Cut down, or, preferably, cut out all the other things in your diet and lifestyle that make your stomach more sensitive. This means alcohol, smoking, caffeine, pickled or fatty foods, and so on. This is a good idea for your general health anyway. You will be amazed at the difference this can make. At the very least, don't take other stomach-irritating foods, or nutritional supplements such as vitamins, at the same time as the extract.

6. Try the glycerine-based extract, which is available from several companies (see list in appendix 1), instead of the alcohol-based extract. It could be the alcohol in the extract that is the problem, not the medicinal substances.

7. Try a flavored extract instead of a plain one (see appendix 1 for where to order this). It may be more palatable for you.

8. Although it's a strong spice, ginger is also a powerful remedy for nausea. Some doctors recommend it for patients who have nausea due to chemotherapy, which is one of the worst kinds of nausea you can have. You can get ginger at grocery stores in the spices section or raw in the produce department. Make a cup of tea with two teaspoons of the grated or powdered root. A glass of ginger ale will also provide the

right dose. In some people, ginger can cause heartburn, though.

9. As a last resort, decrease the daily dose of extract that you're taking.

Side Effect 2: Fatigue

This side effect occurs in about 0.4 percent (1 in 250) of people taking St. John's wort.[6] Other antidepressants cause it too, and we don't know for certain why. With other drugs, the fatigue may be due to their sedative effects. But St. John's wort doesn't have a sedative effect, so we can't explain why some people feel fatigued with it.

PREVENTING FATIGUE

If fatigue occurs, the obvious things to look for would be to see if you're eating and sleeping enough, or getting the right amount of exercise—not too little or too much. I'd recommend cutting out alcohol and caffeine and going for a walk in the sunlight early each morning for thirty minutes to an hour. These simple steps will help set your "body clock" to the proper sleep/wake cycle, meaning you'll be more alert in the day and sleepier at night.

Side Effect 3: Skin Rashes and Itching

In the large drug monitoring study I've been mentioning, skin problems occurred in about 0.3 percent of patients (about 1 in 300). These are particularly interesting side effects to doctors, because we believe we know exactly why they occur.

Hypericin, one of the main active medicinal ingredients of the plant, gives the extract its rich, red color. But it is also a photosensitizer. Cattle and sheep that graze on St. John's wort can become badly sunburned as a result. This is how the plant defends itself from being eaten by hungry animals and insects.

Ranchers are unhappy about this, though, and consider the herb to be a noxious weed. In many countries, including the United States, they've tried to wipe it out with chemical and biological herbicides.

We know that sunburns from the hypericin in St. John's wort only become a problem if animals eat a huge quantity of it—for instance, when it's their main source of food. If it's eaten in normal medicinal amounts, as we humans use it, it's very unlikely to be a problem.[7] Incidentally, I once spoke to an organic farmer who also raised cattle, and he told me that if the animals were eating St. John's wort as their main source of food, then it was just due to bad management by their owners, such as neglecting to give the poor creatures any feed, or keeping the animals in pens that were too small, or overgrazing the land.

In any case, if used in normal medicinal doses, only about 1 in 350 people will become photosensitized by St. John's wort.[8] Herbalists say it occurs most frequently in fair-haired, blue-eyed men, and this makes sense. People without much natural pigment are more susceptible to sunburn than others, and men tend to work in outdoor occupations more often than women. Clearly, you can predict that this side effect will occur if you're fair-complexioned and you get a lot of sun. All of this leads up to the most important point here: You can prevent it.

PREVENTING SKIN PROBLEMS

This is very straightforward: Protect your skin from excessive sunlight. As any dermatologist will tell you, this is a good thing to do whether you're taking St. John's wort or not. Try to stay out of the sun between 10 A.M. and 3 P.M., and wear a hat, long sleeves, and sunscreen. In addition, since the photo-sensitizing effect of hypericin is dose-related, you should use a lower dose of extract in the summer months, especially if you're fair-skinned.

If you start to become sun-sensitive, you are using too high a dose. Cut it down.

Side Effect 4: Anxiety

Anxiety was a reported side effect in 0.26 percent (1 in 400) of people taking St. John's wort extract.[9] As a comparison, anxiety is a much more common side effect of Prozac, affecting about 9 percent (1 in 11) of people taking it.[10] When I've prescribed Prozac, I've sometimes been shocked at how severe the anxiety it causes can be for people. One middle-aged woman, for instance, was virtually unable to leave her room because of the inexplicable terror she felt. It seems to be worst in the first few days, though, and then it passes. In fact, after a week or two, Prozac starts to have a strong *anti*anxiety effect. This is understandable on the basis of the biochemical changes in the brain that we know Prozac causes.

St. John's wort works as an antidepressant in several different ways, as I mentioned in chapter 3. One of them is similar to the way Prozac works, involving interactions with the serotonin levels in the brain. So it's not surprising that it can, in rare cases, produce the same kind of side effects as Prozac. I've never seen it do this, though.

If you do feel anxiety when you use St. John's wort, then, it's likely that it will just be a temporary thing. Decrease the dose until it passes. The antianxiety effect of the herb, as described in chapter 1, will appear within a few weeks.

Side Effect 5: Allergy

Virtually anything can cause an allergic response, and St. John's wort is no exception. About 0.2 percent of people (1 in 500) had an allergic reaction to it in the monitoring study. This category of side effects may have overlapped with the skin problems discussed above, because allergies to medications usually take the form of itchy skin rashes. If a person's stomach and intestines become inflamed from allergic contact with the drug, they can also experience nausea, abdominal pain, and diarrhea. You will notice that these are the same symptoms that were mentioned above, under "Stomach and Intestinal Symptoms," where they were due to nonallergic causes. So it's not always easy to tell if a side effect is due to allergy or to other causes. This is one of the reasons why you should talk to your doctor as soon as possible about any side effect you experience. If a true allergic reaction develops when you're using the extract, you should stop using it.

The most serious kinds of allergic reactions are those where the person's airways swell up and threaten to close off. Theoretically, this can occur with any drug, though there's no reports of it ever happening with St. John's wort. If your lips, tongue, or throat do swell up, however, or if you have difficulty breathing, you need to call an ambulance immediately and be treated in an emergency room.

Side Effect 6: Dizziness

Dizziness occurs in about 0.15 percent of people taking the extract (less than 1 in 650).[11] With most other antidepressants, this is one of their most common side effects—lightheadedness, or "spinning out." It happens because they interfere with the body's mechanisms for regulating blood pressure. The blood pressure becomes too low, so that when a person stands up, there's not enough pressure to pump blood upward from the heart to the brain. The brain doesn't get enough blood, and so the person feels light-headed and dizzy.

This can be a dangerous side effect of antidepressants and other drugs, because it can cause blackouts and falls. In fact, it's a leading cause of hospitalizations amongst older people. When I was an intern, I did a rotation on an orthopedic ward, where we treated broken bones. The single most common type of problem we treated were the broken hips of senior citizens who were taking conventional antidepressants or other drugs that interfered with their blood pressure control. They became dizzy and fell, breaking their fragile hip bones. Sadly, a broken hip is often the beginning of a downward spiral of illness that can be fatal for old people.

Because of this, it's in just that age group that St. John's wort will probably save thousands of lives. It causes dizziness far less often than other drugs.

PREVENTING DIZZINESS

Here are some things you can do to prevent dizziness and falls:

1. Stand up slowly, especially if you've been sitting or lying down for a long time. Standing up slowly, in stages, allows your blood pressure system more time to adapt to the changes in your posture. For example, if you're lying in bed, first rise to a sitting position, and stay there for a minute or two before you stand up.

2. If you feel any dizziness coming on, immediately put your head down as low as you can, for instance, between your knees if you can. More blood will reach your head, and it will prevent a blackout. Then rise up again very slowly, over a period of several minutes.

3. If the dizziness is severe, you should probably stop using the extract. You might do better with a different medication. But because St. John's wort is about as safe as you can get in

terms of medications, you might not have many other options. If you've run out of medication options, some doctors treat low blood pressure with high-pressure stockings that keep the blood from pooling in the legs, with a high-salt diet, and sometimes with drugs that raise blood pressure.

Miscellaneous Rare Side Effects

I'm going to briefly discuss the side effects which occurred in less than 1 in 1,000 patients in the drug monitoring study. You are obviously very unlikely to be troubled by them, but they are as follows:

Dry mouth. (One study reported that this was a fairly common side effect of St. John's wort, occurring in 6 percent of people using it.[12]) Action plan: Carry a water bottle and take frequent small sips.

Sleep disturbances. Action plan: Follow steps listed above under "Fatigue."

Palpitations. Action plan: See your doctor for a physical examination.

Weakness. Action plan: See your doctor for a physical examination.

Worsening of other current illnesses. Action plan: See your doctor.

Finally, one patient out of the 3,250 had real troubles with the extract. He reported tremor, light sensitivity, visual problems, burning eyes, circulatory problems, urinary problems, tension, and euphoria.[13] From this list of symptoms, I would guess that he may have been experiencing a low-grade manic episode—that is, his mood went *too* high. This is what happens to some people with bipolar disorder (manic depression) when they take antidepressants. Instead of just lifting out of their depression, they go sky-high, into a state of high-pressured overactivity and euphoria, which is actually a form of misery in itself. I don't recommend St. John's wort for people with bipolar disorder.

A Final Note on Side Effects

I want to emphasise again that this book is not meant to replace the care of your doctor. If you have any symptoms of depression (see chapter 6 for a list), you should seek the help of a doctor. You should only use St. John's wort under his or her supervision. And please remain alert for side effects, and report them to your doctor immediately. You are unique, and your therapy needs individual attention and care.

Chapter 10

GROW YOUR OWN—
IT'S EASY!

Just Ignore It

There's a secret to growing St. John's wort: Just ignore it. It hates mollycoddling. Just let it do its own thing, and it'll thrive. If your thumbs are anything but green, you'll find you can grow this herb with ease.

You don't need to fertilize it, weed it, prune it, or do any of those other odious garden chores for it. If there's a drought, you might have to water it very occasionally, but that's about it.

An organic grower I spoke to told me he had a greenhouse set up to provide what he thought would be the ideal growing conditions. But did it grow there? No. Instead, it sprouted up right *outside* the greenhouse, all on its own. This plant has its own ideas about how to live.

How to Enjoy Your Plant

In many psychiatric hospitals, including one that I worked in, gardening is used as a form of therapy. Chances are that you'll find that growing St. John's wort is a lot of fun, especially since you'll be doing practically no work. Of course, it's not for everybody.

I recommend against growing and using your own medicine unless you've been stable and essentially in remission from symptoms for six months or so. This is because the dosage of homegrown herbs is more difficult to standardize than that of commercial preparations. You need to be certain you're getting the right dose, especially when you're starting out on a medication.

Where to Grow It

St. John's wort will grow just about anywhere in temperate regions—wet areas, dry ones, you name it. Too much watering, however, will annoy it—it needs soil with some drainage. It likes very poor soil, but it will also grow in rich soil. It prefers full sun, but it doesn't mind a bit of shade, and will even grow on the northern side of buildings in the northern hemisphere. It grows at all elevations, though its yield of oil is not as good at high altitudes.

One of its favorite places to grow is in the torn-up land left behind by loggers, in piles of "slash" (dead branches and other debris). The debris provides some shelter for its roots. It's also especially fond of spots where gophers have dug up the earth.

So if you're interested in growing it, select the place in your garden that is the most disrupted and has the poorest soil. If the drainage is poor there, you can improve it by putting down a border of railway ties or rocks and filling up the inside with soil. Then toss some branches or bark chips over the soil. The bed should be about a foot deep and three feet wide.

Then you're ready to plant it. Late fall or early spring are the best times. You can buy small organically grown plants at nurseries and herb shops. Some organic food stores carry herb seedlings, too, or will order them in for you. Make sure they're organically grown, since nonorganic seedlings are not as hardy. They've already been mollycoddled with fertilizers and pesticides.

Or you can grow it from seed yourself. According to Ted Snider, farm manager at the Eclectic Institute in Oregon, there's a trick to doing this. "Make believe it's on the side of the road," he says. "Don't treat it nicely. Just throw the seed on the ground, give it some water, and leave it alone."

At the Eclectic Institute, they've experimented with growing St. John's wort in neat rows in their fields, as is normal for most other types of crops. They've discovered that if it's cultivated in this way, however, it poses an attractive target for beetles. The beetles can kill it, but more commonly they just prevent it from setting buds. When the plant grows in the wild, in nature's disorderly splendor, it's much more resistant to beetles. You can simulate a natural setting by not planting it in large quantities on its own. Put other types of plants around it. Make sure the other plants are far enough away from it, however, so that their roots do not take away nourishment from its patch of soil.

Actually, growing different types of plants together is one of the basic principles of organic gardening. It's the fact that we grow huge mono-crops of plants such as wheat and cotton all in one place that makes them so vulnerable to attack by insects, fungi, and so on. And that's why farmers have to spray them with poisons. In addition, mono-crops deplete the soil of nutrients to a much greater degree than do mixed crops. But I digress.

How to Ignore Your Plant

There are really just two things you can do to help your St. John's wort once it's established: Water it during droughts and cover it with a sheet on frosty nights. Freezing or total desiccation will kill it.

The plant will grow to be about three to four inches tall in the first year. It will look good until winter comes, and then it will die back to a little clump of woody stems. This is normal. It will look a little more straggly in the following years, but it will produce more buds. See chapter 2 for information on when and how to harvest it, and how to prepare your own extract.

The plant will live for several years. The average size is between one and two feet tall for mature specimens, but particularly healthy ones can reach three and a half feet. It's claimed to be highly invasive, but organic farmers deny this. It won't take over unless the land is severely damaged, as through overgrazing. Still, it's listed as a "Class B Noxious Weed" in many areas, and your local nonorganic farmers and grazers might be unhappy about your growing it.

Can I Grow It Indoors?

Yes! You will need to pay more attention to it, though, as it will be entirely at your mercy. Plant the seedlings in wide, shallow pots, in a mixture of two parts peat, two parts garden soil, one part compost or composted manure, and one part sand. Water them in. Then only water them when the soil becomes dry.

They'll need as much sunlight as they can get—at least six hours daily. An electric grow-light would help.

Happy growing!

Suppliers of Seeds

Seeds of Change
PO Box 15700
Santa Fe, NM 87506-5700
Phone toll free: 1-888-762-7333
Fax toll free: 1-888-329-4762

Organically grown, open-pollinated, heirloom variety; 100 seeds for $2.29 plus postage. Will ship internationally.

Seed Savers Exchange
3076 North Winn Rd.
Decorah, IA 52101
Phone or fax: 1-319-382-5872

The Seed Savers Exchange is a nonprofit organization with 8,000 members who are rescuing "heirloom" (handed-down) varieties of vegetables, fruits, grains, flowers, and herbs from extinction. This work is critically important for the earth's ecosystem, as the diversity of the plants we humans grow is diminishing every year. You probably didn't know, for example, that there are literally hundreds of different kinds of apples and potatoes. Only a few are offered in most supermarkets—generic, often genetically altered varieties. The rest of the natural varieties would become extinct if not for groups like this one. Membership costs $7 a year, and apart from helping to save the earth, it entitles you to purchase seeds directly from other members at a very minimal cost. Although St. John's wort is not in danger of extinction, a number of Seed Saver Exchange members grow it, and you can buy it from them.

Chapter 11

THE EARTH'S OWN MEDICINE

St. John's wort is one of the most widespread plants in the world. It so abundant and hardy that it is one of the commonest "weeds" in places like California, South Africa, and Australia.

Any herbalist will tell you that the word "weed" is really a misnomer. The word means "a useless plant," and there is no such thing. Many so-called weeds contain some of the best medicines available. A tea made of nettles, for example, a "weed" that grows by roadsides throughout the northern hemisphere, provides effective relief from hay fever. And dandelions can help fight liver disease.

Ranchers around the world dislike St. John's wort, though. Their sheep and cattle sometimes eat it in large quantities, causing the animals to become badly sunburned. (As I mentioned in chapter 9, this effect usually only occurs when the herb is a main source of food.)

Because of these unhappy ranchers, the governments of

Canada, Australia, and South Africa are busily funding projects to find some way to wipe out St. John's wort! Even as you read this, they are trying out new chemical and biological herbicides to kill it off.[1,2] In the United States, too, the Department of Agriculture has been trying unsuccessfully to eliminate it for the last fifty years or so.[3]

This is amazing to me. It really illustrates the crazy lengths to which we will go to maintain our environmentally destructive way of life. It's the *ranching* that is the problem for the environment, not the St. John's wort.

Ranching, for example, is the single biggest cause of the serious ecological devastation that Australia has experienced since it was colonized by white people two hundred years ago. Before the white people came, the native plants had become adapted to living in a land of soft-footed animals, such as kangaroos. The plants' root systems were shallow, spread out near the surface of the soil to catch the scanty rain. When herds of hard-footed sheep and cattle were introduced, they broke up the soil and damaged the fragile root systems. The native plants now have trouble surviving. The result has been the destruction of much of the landscape of Australia.

Traveling through the ranching areas of Australia is an education about environmental vandalism. The native plants there are most often weak, dead, or completely gone. Instead, foreign species that are able to survive the effects of the herds grow everywhere. In Australia's arid Northern Territory, for example, an exotic species of thorn bush has taken over much of the land. The thorns are so sharp and difficult to remove from the coats of sheep that the poor animals get tangled up in them and cut by them, and die from skin infections. In fact, huge areas of northern Australia, as large as American states or European countries, are so infested with the thorn bushes that virtually all the sheep there became sick and died, and the ranchers simply had to leave. The land has been placed under quarantine, to prevent travelers from spreading the thorn bushes' seeds. Now that it's free of the ranchers, the land is slowly recovering its balance.

I've spoken to people in ranching communities in Australia, and they know full well that they're destroying the land. But Australian beef fetches a high price around the world, and this is how they make their living. They're like the loggers in California or the whalers in Japan. To them, if it's how they make their money, somehow it must be okay. And so of course, they also feel justified in trying to wipe out the "weeds" that hurt their herds, such as thorns and St. John's wort.

This exact sequence of environmental damage has occurred in many areas of the world. Most of the Middle East, for instance, was once a lush, well-vegetated landscape. Thousands of years of overgrazing have turned it into the thorny and bramble-filled desert that it is today. And the "weed" St. John's wort now flourishes there.

In the dry western United States, too, overgrazing has had a major impact. True, herds of wild animals such as buffalo had always grazed there. These wild herds migrated throughout the year, however, covering vast ranges of land. This cycle of migration had allowed the land to rest for several months each year and recover from grazing, and had maintained the healthy balance of nature. But the white settlers with their domesticated herds disregarded the cycles of nature, and overran the carrying capacities of the land. They kept their animals on the same land year-round. They grazed their animals on fragile, sparsely vegetated land that the wild herds would have avoided. By the early 1900s, the ecology of the dry American rangelands had been seriously disturbed.

It was exactly at this time that the population of St. John's wort began to explode. It sprang up densely throughout the low-elevation valleys, canyons, and plains—the very places that had been overgrazed. In some areas of California, St. John's wort displaced virtually all of the other plants, making grazing impossible.[4] There are remarkable old photographs of Californian grazing land completely blanketed with St. John's wort.

Ranchers were in despair. They watched as their herds dwindled and their profits disappeared. They tried to control the herb using herbicides and by planting other forage crops, but nothing worked. So in 1945, the U.S. Department of Agriculture stepped in, launching a massive campaign to eradicate St. John's wort. They imported several species of beetles from France to do the job, and distributed them throughout the country. This biological means of control proved more effective. By 1956, the population of St. John's wort had been significantly reduced.[5]

It still flourishes in the western United States today, however, especially in the Pacific Northwest, and ranchers there still consider it a plague. To this day, 4-H clubs (children's agricultural clubs) in some American ranching communities continue to organize anti–St. John's wort projects. For example, they send the children on bus trips to distribute beetles to areas "infested" with the herb. The ranchers' battle with nature goes on.

Ranching doesn't just disturb the ecology of the dry grasslands of the world. It also fuels the destruction of the earth's rain forests. Throughout South America, Southeast Asia, and elsewhere, they are being cleared to make way for grazing land. We want more meat on our tables, and so the forests must go.

Some ecologists talk about "the will of the land," referring to the ability of ecosystems to protect themselves from damage, and even heal themselves. In Australia and California, you can see this will in action. Hardy plants such as St. John's wort and thorns proliferate when the land is stressed, and the other species vanish. These so-called "weeds" survive because they have defenses against sheep and cattle. If you look at it in another way, by growing plants with defenses like these, the land is actually protecting itself from the ranching. These plants set limits on the number of sheep and cattle that the land will permit to graze there. In parts of northern Australia and California, the land has even completely banished the ranchers. Thorns and St. John's wort are part of the earth's own self-healing mechanisms.

Perhaps in an even larger sense, the earth itself is saying that it's had enough of ranching. Our human desire to eat large amounts of meat is unhealthy both for the earth and for our own bodies. And we also massively overproduce wool. Australia, for instance, has huge stockpiles of wool that it can't sell at any price, because the world market is flooded. The government has to subsidize the wool industry so that it won't totally collapse.

If you want to live in harmony with the "will of the land," and help the earth survive, probably the single most effective thing that you can do is to cut down on your meat consumption. It's no coincidence, too, that this is also one of the best ways to stay physically healthy and live longer. The things that are good for the earth are also good for you.

The healing forces of the earth can also heal you. St. John's wort is a prime example of this—a powerful medicine both for the land and for human beings. It heals the land from the devastation caused by our twentieth-century consumer way of life. And it heals us on an individual level, from illnesses such as depression—illnesses due, in part, to that very same stressful and toxic way of life.

There is nothing mystical or magical about this—it just makes good biological sense. We human beings evolved as an integral part of the environment of this planet, and we remain an integral part of it. Though we try to deny it, and build an artificial shell around ourselves, we are all still deeply connected to the earth.

Our food, the water we drink, the air we breathe, the petrochemical fuels we burn, the medicines we use, and all of our activities link us with the lives of every other living thing around us. We cannot separate our own health from the over-all health of the planet.

Most people would define the word "health" as "the absence of disease." Perhaps we should add to this definition: *living in harmony with the will of the earth.*

Appendix 1

SUPPLIERS OF ST. JOHN'S WORT

Liquid Extracts (or Tinctures)

Here's a list of some of the suppliers of extract and where you can contact them. It's divided into sections for the United States, the United Kingdom, Europe, and Australia. This list is not comprehensive. I don't recommend one of them over any of the others. However, if you are allergic to corn or grains, you might do best to use the Eclectic Institute's hypoallergenic extract. If you're a strict vegetarian, you might want to use Nature's Answer, since they use vegetable glycerine (not animal glycerine) in the extraction process. Their product is also certified to be kosher. Some companies call their product a tincture. This means that it is an alcohol-based extract.

UNITED STATES

Eclectic Institute
Sandy, Oregon 97055-9549
Phone: 1-800-332-4372
Fax: 1-503-668-3227

Organic, hypoallergenic—without corn or grain alcohol. Available in plain or black cherry flavor, with Vitamin C.

Gaia Herbs
Harvard, MA 01451
Phone: 1-800-831-7780
Fax: 1-800-717-1722

Extracted from flowers and buds only.

Herb Pharm
Williams, OR 97544
Phone: 1-800-348-4372
Fax: 1-800-545-7392

Extracted from flowers and buds only.

McZand Herbal
PO Box 5312
Santa Monica CA 90409
Phone: 1-800-800-0405
Fax: 1-310-822-1050

This extract is a little more expensive than most, but it appears to be more concentrated.

Nature's Answer
Hauppage, NY 11788

Ask your health food store owner to order it for you—no sales directly to the public. Alcohol-free extract, with vegetable glycerine.

Nature's Plus
548 Broadhollow Rd.
Melville, NY 11747
Phone: 1-800-645-9500
Fax: 1-516-249-2022

This extract is standardized, and made with vegetable glycerine.

Planetary Formulations
PO Box 533
Soquel, CA 95073
Phone: 1-800-776-7701
Fax: 1-408-438-7410

A more concentrated extract than most. Manufacturer recommends taking it three days on, two days off.

CANADA

Canadians can order from U.S. suppliers. Alternatively, here's a Canadian supplier of extracts and capsules who will also ship anywhere:

Health Service Center
971 Bloor St. West
Toronto, Ontario 46H1L7
Phone or fax: 1-416-535-9562

UNITED KINGDOM

Baldwin's
173 Walworth Rd.
London SE 17 1RW
Phone: 44-0171-703-5550

EUROPE

In German-speaking countries, St. John's wort extract is available both by prescription and as an over-the-counter medication. Ask for it at your local doctor's, pharmacy, or health food store. Some of the trade names are Esbericum, Hyperforat, Jarsin, Neurapas, Neuroplant, Psychotonin M, and Sedariston. Here is a manufacturer of capsules containing extract:

Lichtwer Pharma GmbH.
Berlin, Germany
Phone: 49-30-403-700

AUSTRALIA

Many Australian suppliers will not sell directly to the public. You may have to ask your health food store owner or doctor/naturopath to order it for you. Here are two companies who will sell extract directly to you:

Herbal Supplies Pty. Ltd.
1–5 Jennifer Ave.
Ridgehaven, South Australia
Phone: 61-08-8264-2453 or 08-8265-4777
Fax: 61-08-8263-2033

MediHerb
124 McEvoy St.
Warwick, Queensland 4370
Phone: 61-07-661-0700
Fax: 61-07-661-5656

Capsules (United States)

Depending on the brand, capsules of St. John's wort may be considerably less expensive than the extract. However, capsules are not the best form to take—see chapter 7 for further details.

Nutrition Headquarters, Inc.
One Nutrition Plaza
Carbondale, IL 62901-8825
Fax: 1-618-529-4553

Postal or fax orders only.

Guaranteed potency herb; capsules standardized for hyper-icin content.

Eclectic Institute.

See page 126 for address and phone number. Freeze-dried herbal extracts. These capsules are not standardized.

Hypericum Buyers Club
8205 Santa Monica Boulevard, Suite 472
Los Angeles, CA 90046
Phone: 1-888-497-3742

The supplier states that these capsules are the same type that were used in most of the studies on depression.

Appendix 2

CONVENTIONAL ANTIDEPRESSANT MEDICATIONS

The Place for Conventional Drugs

Sometimes, conventional antidepressant medications are indispensable. They can help the severely depressed in times when they're literally too depressed for any other sort of therapy. They might not be able to concentrate enough for psychotherapy or even relaxation therapy. Or they might have tried all the other treatments with limited effect, and in getting past the block might need an extra push.

Taking into account both its effectiveness and low number of side effects, St. John's wort performs better than conventional drugs in *mild* depression. At present, however, there have been no studies on the use of St. John's wort in *severe* depression. True, there are some early indications that it may work just as well for severe cases. But until actual studies have been done on this, we need to play it safe and restrict its use to mild depression.

The Choices

There are three main types of conventional antidepressant medications: The SRIs, such as Prozac and Zoloft; the cyclic antidepressants, including Tofranil and Elavil; and the MAOIs, such as Parnate and Nardil. There are other types, too, including Desyrel, Wellbutrin, and Effexor. In addition, many new drugs have recently been developed, and they may well make these other choices obsolete in the next decade or so.

Each type of drug has a different set of side effects, but they all share some common characteristics: They relieve the symptoms of depression in about 60 to 80 percent of people who use them, and they take four to six weeks to produce their full effects.

The different groups of antidepressants each affect a slightly different set of chemicals in the brain. Since the chemistry of every person's brain is unique, a person might do better with a particular type of drug than with the others. Usually, it's a matter of trial and error to find the one that's right for the individual. If a given drug is going to be helpful, it should have produced a beneficial effect by the fourth week or so. If it hasn't worked by then, a different drug can be tried.

The choice of which drug to use first is usually based on which set of side effects the person is willing to put up with. A person who is very restless at night, for instance, might be more willing to take Desyrel, since it causes drowsiness. They will probably not want Prozac, because it can make restlessness worse. This is the sort of reasoning that psychiatrists use when they prescribe antidepressants.

Antidepressants produce their effects in an interesting way—they start with the body, and then only gradually begin to affect the mind and emotions. So the first symptoms to improve—usually starting around the tenth day—are the physical symptoms, such as fatigue, insomnia, and loss of appetite. Then the low mood begins to lift.

Prozac and the Other SRIs

SRIs (serotonin reuptake inhibitors) such as Prozac (fluoxetine) or Zoloft (sertraline) are currently recommended as first-line drugs. Prozac was introduced in 1988, and has become the most widely used antidepressant in the United States. Actually, classifying it as an antidepressant is a little misleading. It's used not only for the treatment of depression, but also for a wide range of other psychiatric diagnoses, including eating disorders, anxiety disorders, and even personality disorders. In addition, many people take it who do not really have a psychiatric illness. They use it as a means to help them adapt to the stresses of everyday life—although this type of use is not officially sanctioned.

Recently, attention has focused on the possible ability of Prozac to change people's personality toward becoming more extroverted and confident. This may or may not be true. Many believe it is a placebo effect. Prozac affects the serotonin system in the brain, however, and we know that serotonin is important for the way that the brain handles social behavior. Altering a person's levels of serotonin with drugs like Prozac may make the person feel less sensitive to rejection and more willing to take social risks. Our society rewards people who are willing to take social risks—to be outgoing and thick-skinned, like salespeople and movie stars. That's one of the reasons why Prozac is so popular.

As I discussed in chapter 3, one of the ways that St. John's wort works is through the serotonin system, much like Prozac. It can therefore also provide the same effects of general stress reduction and of shielding us from feelings of social anxiety. Many Europeans take a sip of it each morning, for just these reasons.

SRIs such as Prozac are sometimes referred to as "low toxicity" antidepressants. In reality, they are only "low toxicity" when compared to the older types of antidepressants, which were very toxic indeed. Prozac has many side effects. Some of them are severe. In fact, I've seen more than one patient who was seriously poisoned by Prozac.

The common side effects of SRIs (using Prozac as an example) are as follows: nausea (in 21 percent of cases), headache (20 percent), nervousness (15 percent), insomnia (14 percent), weight loss (13 percent), drowsiness (12 percent), diarrhea (12 percent), dry mouth (10 percent), loss of appetite, anxiety, tremor, dizziness, stomach upset, and excessive sweating (all less than 10 percent). Less common side effects include loss of the ability to have an orgasm, the development of various types of rashes, and a decrease in blood glucose (therefore diabetics should use it with care). Recently, it's been discovered that Prozac also decreases melatonin levels in the body—which is a real worry, considering that melatonin not only keeps our body clock regular, but that it also has an important anticancer effect.

In the late 1980s there were widely publicized reports that Prozac was linked to an increased likelihood of violent acts such as suicide and homicide, but many subsequent reviews have clearly proved that no such association exists.

Tofranil and the Other Cyclics

The cyclic group of antidepressants, which include Tofranil (imipramine), Elavil (amitriptyline), and Sinequan (doxepin), are the oldest group in use, dating back to the 1950s. Tofranil is still considered to represent the "gold standard" in antidepressant effectiveness—all others are compared to it to determine how well they work.

In terms of side effects, however, the cyclic antidepressants have by far the worst record. They cause serious side effects with monotonous regularity, especially in patients over the age of 65. Because they interfere with the control of blood pressure, they frequently cause blackouts, which can lead to falls and hip fractures. The drowsiness they cause also leads to accidents, and makes it risky to drive or operate heavy machinery. In some patients, they also cause serious abnormalities of the heart's rhythm.

Despite all this, the tricyclics are still the standard type of antidepressant used by many doctors, mainly because they're inexpensive. Health maintenance organizations (HMOs), especially, encourage their use as a cost-cutting measure.

The common side effects of the cyclic antidepressants vary from individual drug to drug, but in general they are, in rough order of occurrence from most frequent to least: sedation, dry mouth and postural hypotension (which causes dizziness on standing up, and may lead to blackouts and falls), nausea, constipation or diarrhea, weight gain, blurred vision, difficulty with urination, increased heart rate, palpitations, sweating, rashes, impotence, confusion, and, rarely, a drop in the white blood cell count (which can lead to serious infections), hepatitis, increased blood pressure, and heart arrhythmias.

Unless there's some very good reason for you to take a cyclic antidepressant, I would suggest you use a different kind.

The MAOIs

MAOIs (monoamine oxidase inhibitors) are used less frequently than the other types. Nardil (phenelzine) is an example of an older MAOI, and Aurorix (moclobemide) is one of the newer ones. They are considered to be particularly effective for so-called atypical depression, that is, depression with symptoms of overeating, oversleeping, and anxiety. The common side effects of MAOIs are postural hypotension (causing dizziness on standing up, which can lead to blackouts and falls), weight gain, swollen ankles, impotence or other loss of sexual functioning, and insomnia.

MAOIs may also cause dangerous elevations of blood pressure if the person eats foods containing the amino acid tyramine. As a result, people taking these drugs need to be on a restricted diet. (See chapter 6 for a list of the restricted foods.) If you're a careful person, and are willing to put up with all of the restrictions, though, MAOIs are not a bad choice, since they're usually pretty well tolerated.

Desyrel

Desyrel (trazodone) is a newer antidepressant, and is already quite commonly used in the United States. It causes drowsiness, so many doctors prescribe it as a sleeping aid for depressed people. Since Prozac causes insomnia in many people, Desyrel is sometimes used along with it. Apart from drowsiness, it can cause dizziness, headache, low blood pressure, dry mouth, and upset stomach. In rare cases, it causes a prolonged erection in men. That can severely damage the penis and lead to impotence.

Wellbutrin

Wellbutrin (bupropion) is a unique antidepressant that is similar to amphetamine ("speed") in its chemical structure. Although it was initially withdrawn from use because it caused seizures, it seems to be safe for most people. It doesn't affect the heart as many other antidepressants do, so it is good for treating depression in people with heart problems. Like

amphetamines, though, it commonly causes insomnia, restlessness, irritability, and headache.

Effexor

Effexor (venlafaxine) is very similar to a natural antidepressant chemical found in chocolate called phenylethylamine. (Yes, chocolate is a natural antidepressant food!)

Effexor's main advantage is that it is said to work faster than other antidepressants. Side effect–wise, a whopping 37 percent of patients report that it makes them feel nauseated, and around 20 percent say it makes them feel drowsy, dizzy, or dry in the mouth. The most serious side effect it causes is an increase in blood pressure, so if you already have high blood pressure, this isn't the drug for you.

References:

P.A. Childs et al. Effect of fluoxetine on melatonin in patients with seasonal affective disorder and matched controls. *Br J Psychiatry* 166, no. 2 (1995): 196–8.

H.I. Kaplan, B.J. Sadock, and J.A. Grebb. *Kaplan and Sadock's Synopsis of Psychiatry,* 7th ed. (Baltimore: Williams and Wilkins, 1994).

P.D. Kramer. *Listening to Prozac.* (New York: Viking, 1993).

Appendix 3

HOW TO FIND A DOCTOR WHO PRACTICES HOLISTIC MEDICINE

Holistic Medicine

To locate a medical doctor in your area who practices according to the principles of holistic medicine, call or write to:

> American Holistic Medical Association
> 4101 Lake Boone Trail, Suite 201
> Raleigh, NC 27607
> Phone: 1-919-787-5146 (ask for the referral line).

For $5, you will be sent a listing of holistic physicians across the United States. This takes four to six weeks.

Naturopathic Medicine

Naturopaths, or N.D.s, offer an alternative to conventional medicine. They've kept alive a lot of natural healing techniques that otherwise might have been left by the wayside.

Naturopaths employ a variety of treatments, including nutritional therapy, herbalism, homeopathy, acupuncture, and physical manipulation. They are not allowed to prescribe conventional drugs, but most of them would prefer not to anyway.

Naturopaths are now regulated in many states. In the past, the standard of naturopathic education was poor, but recently, it has been making strides and gaining wide respect.

Naturopathic medicine is particularly good for treating chronic illnesses where conventional medicine has failed. Naturopaths are usually less adept at diagnosis than conventional doctors, however. You're better off seeing a conventional doctor or a holistic doctor (see above) to get a firm diagnosis before you consult a naturopath. Unfortunately, only one or two insurance companies will pay for their services.

To locate a good naturopathic physician in your area, contact:

American Association of Naturopathic Physicians
2366 Eastlake Avenue East, Suite 322
Seattle, WA 98102
Phone: 1-206-827-6035
Fax: 1-206-323-7612

For $5, they'll mail you some brochures on naturopathic medicine, along with a list of licensed naturopaths across the United States.

Appendix 4

FOR THE HEALTH PROFESSIONAL: REVIEW ARTICLES ON ST. JOHN'S WORT

There have been dozens of published clinical studies on the use of St. John's wort in depression. The following articles each provide a review, critique, and summary of these studies:

G. Harrer and V. Schulz. Clinical investigation of the antidepressant effectiveness of Hypericum. *Journal of Geriatric Psychiatry and Neurology* 7 Suppl. 1 (1994): S 6–8.

E. Ernst. St. John's wort, an antidepressant—a systematic, criteria-based review. *Phytomedicine* 2, no. 1 (1995): 67–71.

K. Linde et al. St. John's wort for depression—an overview and meta-analysis of randomised clinical trials. *British Medical Journal* 313, no. 7052 (1996): 253–8.

REFERENCES

Chapter 1. How St. John's Wort Can Help You

1. See refs. 1–13 in chapter 3.
2. B. Martinez, S. Kasper, S. Ruhrmann, and H.J. Moller. Hypericum in the treatment of seasonal affective disorders. *Journal of Geriatric Psychiatry and Neurology* 7 Suppl. 1(1994): S 29–33.
3. H. Woelk, G. Burkard, and J. Grunwald. Benefits and risks of the hypericum extract LI 160: drug monitoring study with 3250 patients. *Journal of Geriatric Psychiatry and Neurology* 7 Suppl. 1(1994): S 34–8.
4. M.A. Jenike. Hypericum: a novel antidepressant (editorial). *Journal of Geriatric Psychiatry and Neurology* 7 Suppl. 1(1994): S 1.
5. B. Thiele, I. Brink, and M. Ploch. Modulation of cytokine expression by hypericum extract. *Journal of Geriatric Psychiatry and Neurology* 7 Suppl. 1(1994): S 60–2.

6. See references 4, 12, and 13 in chapter 3.

7. U. Schmidt and H. Sommer. [St. John's wort in the ambulatory treatment of depression. Attention and reaction ability are preserved.] *Fortschritte Der Medizin* 111, no. 19(1993): 339–42.

8. S. Perovic and W.E.G. Muller. [Pharmacological profile of Hypericum extract: Effect on serotonin uptake by postsynaptic receptors.] *Arzneimittel-Forschung* 45, no. 11(1995): 1145–1148.

9. W.E.G. Muller and R. Rossol. Effects of hypericum extract on the expression of serotonin receptors. *Journal of Geriatric Psychiatry and Neurology* 7 Suppl. 1(1994): S 63–4.

10. H. Sommer and G. Harrer. Placebo-controlled double-blind study examining the effectiveness of an hypericum preparation in 105 mildly depressed patients. *Journal of Geriatric Psychiatry and Neurology* 7 Suppl. 1(1994): S 9–11.

11. G. Lavie et al. The chemical and biological properties of hypericin—compound with a broad spectrum of biological activities. *Medicinal Research Reviews* 15, no. 2(1995): 111–9. See also chapter 4.

12. A.G. Kolesnikova. [Bactericidal and immunocorrective properties of plant extracts.] *Zhurnal Mikrobiologii, Epidemiologii I Immunobiologii* no. 3(1986): 75–8. See also chapter 4.

13. T. Shipochliev, A. Dimitrov, and E. Aleksandrova. [Anti-inflammatory action of a group of plant extracts.]

Veterinarno-Meditsinski Nauki. 18, no. 6, 87–94. See also chapter 4.

14. See "A Cure for Cancer?" in chapter 4.

15. H. Wagner and S. Bladt. Pharmaceutical quality of Hypericum extracts. *Journal of Geriatric Psychiatry and Neurology* 7 Suppl 1(1994): 65–8.

16. E.U. Vorbach, W.D. Hubner, and K.H. Arnoldt. Effectiveness and tolerance of the hypericum extract LI 160 in comparison with imipramine: randomized double-blind study with 135 outpatients. *Journal of Geriatric Psychiatry and Neurology* 7 Suppl. 1(1994): S 19–23.

17. G. Harrer, W.D. Hubner, and H. Podzuweit. Effectiveness and tolerance of the hypericum extract LI 160 compared to maprotiline: a multicenter double-blind study. *Journal of Geriatric Psychiatry and Neurology* 7 Suppl. 1(1994): S 24–8.

18. See 3.

Chapter 2. What Is St. John's Wort?

1. N.K.B. Robson. Parallel evolution in tropical montane Hypericum. *Opera Botanica* 0, no. 121(1993): 263–274.

2. M. Castleman. *The Healing Herbs* (Melbourne, Australia: Schwartz Books, 1991), 321–325.

3. M.J. Lohse and B. Muller-Oerlinghausen. Psychopharmaka. In: U. Schwabe and D. Paffrath, eds. *Arzneiverordnungsreport '94* (Stuttgart, Germany: Gustav Fischer, 1994), 354–70.

Chapter 3. St. John's Wort Works—Here's the Proof

1. G. Harrer and V. Schulz. Clinical investigation of the antidepressant effectiveness of hypericum. *Journal of Geriatric Psychiatry and Neurology* 7 Suppl. 1(1994): S 6–8.

2. K. Linde et al. St. John's wort for depression—an overview and meta-analysis of randomised clinical trials. *British Medical Journal* 313, no. 7052(1996): 253–8.

3. E. Ernst. St. John's wort, an antidepressant—a systematic, criteria-based review. *Phytomedicine* 2, no. 1(1995): 67–71.

4. H. Sommer and G. Harrer. Placebo-controlled double-blind study examining the effectiveness of an hypericum preparation in 105 mildly depressed patients. *Journal of Geriatric Psychiatry and Neurology* 7 Suppl. 1(1994): S 9–11.

5. W.D. Hubner, S. Lande, and H. Podzuweit. Hypericum treatment of mild depressions with somatic symptoms. *Journal of Geriatric Psychiatry and Neurology* 7 Suppl. 1(1994): S 12–4.

6. K.D. Hansgen, J. Vesper, and M. Ploch. Multicenter double-blind study examining the antidepressant effectiveness of the hypericum extract LI 160. *Journal of Geriatric Psychiatry and Neurology* 7 Suppl. 1(1994): S 15–8.

7. E.U. Vorbach, W.D. Hubner, and K.H. Arnoldt. Effectiveness and tolerance of the hypericum extract LI 160 in comparison with imipramine: randomized double-blind

study with 135 outpatients. *Journal of Geriatric Psychiatry and Neurology* 7 Suppl. 1(1994): S 19–23.

8. G. Harrer, W.D. Hubner, and H. Podzuweit. Effectiveness and tolerance of the hypericum extract LI 160 compared to maprotiline: a multicenter double-blind study. *Journal of Geriatric Psychiatry and Neurology* 7 Suppl. 1(1994): S 24–8.

9. B. Martinez, S. Kasper, S. Ruhrmann, and H.J. Moller. Hypericum in the treatment of seasonal affective disorders. *Journal of Geriatric Psychiatry and Neurology* 7 Suppl. 1(1994): S 29–33.

10. H. Woelk, G. Burkard, and J. Grunwald. Benefits and risks of the hypericum extract LI 160: drug monitoring study with 3250 patients. *Journal of Geriatric Psychiatry and Neurology* 7 Suppl. 1(1994): S 34–8.

11. U. Schmidt and H. Sommer. [St. John's wort in the ambulatory treatment of depression. Attention and reaction ability are preserved.] *Fortschritte Der Medizin* 111, no. 19(1993): 339–42.

12. B. Witte et al. [Treatment of depressive symptoms with a high concentration hypericum preparation. A multicenter placebo-controlled double-blind study.] *Fortschritte Der Medizin* 113, no. 28(1995): 404–8.

13. H. Muldner and M. Zoller. [Antidepressive effect of a hypericum extract standardized to an active hypericine complex. Biochemical and clinical studies.] *Arzneimittel-Forschung* 34(8): (1984): 918–20.

14. See 7.

15. Ibid.

16. See 2.

17. See 3.

18. See 4, 7, 10, 13.

19. See 9.

20. See 4.

21. See 4, 12, 13.

22. See 4.

23. See 1.

24. See 11.

25. D. Johnson et al. Effects of hypericum extract LI 160 compared with maprotiline on resting EEG and evoked potentials in 24 volunteers. *Journal of Geriatric Psychiatry and Neurology* 7 Suppl. 1(1994): S 44–6.

26. H. Schulz and M. Jobert. Effects of hypericum extract on the sleep EEG in older volunteers. *Journal of Geriatric Psychiatry and Neurology* 7 Suppl. 1(1994): S 39–43.

27. See 10.

28. H.I. Kaplan, B.J. Sadock, and J.A. Grebb. *Kaplan and Sadock's Synopsis of Psychiatry,* 7th ed. (Baltimore: Williams and Wilkins, 1994), 978.

29. J.P. Feighner et al. Comparison of alprazolam, imipramine, and placebo in the treatment of depression. *Journal of the American Medical Association* 249, no. 22(1983): 3057–64.

30. See 7.

31. See 2, 4, 7, 12.

32. H. Wagner and S. Bladt. Pharmaceutical quality of Hypericum extracts. *Journal of Geriatric Psychiatry and Neurology* 7 Suppl 1(1994): 65–8.

33. S. Perovic and W.E.G. Muller. [Pharmacological profile of Hypericum extract: Effect on serotonin uptake by postsynaptic receptors.] *Arzneimittel-Forschung* 45, no. 11(1995): 1145–1148.

34. W.E.G. Mueller and R. Rossol. Effects of hypericum extract on the expression of serotonin receptors. *Journal of Geriatric Psychiatry and Neurology* 7 Suppl. 1(1994): S 63–4.

35. O. Suzuki et al. Inhibition of monoamine oxidase by hypericin. *Planta Medica* 50, no. 3(1984): 272–4.

36. H.M. Thiele and A. Walper. Inhibition of MAO and COMT by hypericum extracts and hypericin. *Journal of Geriatric Psychiatry and Neurology* 7 Suppl. 1(1994): S 54–6.

37. S. Bladt and H. Wagner. Inhibition of MAO by fractions of and constituents of hypericum extract. *Journal of Geriatric Psychiatry and Neurology* 7 Suppl. 1(1994): S 57–9.

38. T.B. Herbert and S. Cohen. Depression and immunity: a meta-analytic review. *Psychological Bulletin* 113, no. 3(1993): 472–486.

39. M. Maes et al. Relationships between interleukin-6 activity, acute phase proteins, and function of the hypothalamic-pituitary-adrenal axis in severe depression. *Psychiatry Research* 49, no. 1(1993): 11–27.

40. B. Thiele, I. Brink, and M. Ploch. Modulation of cytokine expression by hypericum extract. *Journal of Geriatric Psychiatry and Neurology* 7 Suppl. 1(1994): S 60–2.

Chapter 4. St. John's Wort Can Heal Your Body, Too

1. Quoted in: *The New Encyclopedia Brittanica,* 15th ed., vol. 9, pp. 134–5.
2. G. Lavie et al. The chemical and biological properties of hypericin—compound with a broad spectrum of biological activities. *Medicinal Research Reviews* 15, no. 2(1995): 111–9.
3. D. Meruelo, G. Lavie, and D. Lavie. Therapeutic agents with dramatic antiretroviral activity and little toxicity at effective doses: aromatic polycyclic diones hypericin and pseudohypericin. *Proceedings of the National Academy of Sciences of the United States of America* 85, no. 14(1988): 5230–4.
4. See 2.
5. G. Lavie et al. Hypericin as an inactivator of infectious viruses in blood components. *Transfusion* 35, no. 5(1995): 392–400.
6. VIMRx Pharmaceuticals, Inc., press release, Wilmington, DE, 1997.
7. Ibid.
8. M. Capitanio, E.M. Cappelletti, and R. Filippini. Traditional antileukodermic herbal remedies in the Mediter-

ranean area. *Journal of Ethnopharmacology* 27, nos. 1–2(1989): 193–211.

9. A. Nowak, A. Woyton, and E. Baran. [Photodynamic action of extractum hyperici in the treatment of vitiligo.] *Przeglad Dermatologiczny* 61, no. 1(1974): 77–82.

10. J.B. Hudson, I. Lopez-Bazzocchi, and G.H. Towers. Antiviral activities of hypericin. *Antiviral Research* 15, no. 2(1991): 101–12.

11. J.B. Hudson, L. Harris, and G. H. Towers. The importance of light in the anti-HIV effect of hypericin. *Antiviral Research* 20, no. 2(1993): 173–8.

12. S. Carpenter et al. Chemiluminescent activation of the antiviral activity of hypericin: a molecular flashlight. *Proceedings of the National Academy of Sciences of the United States of America* 91, no. 25(1994): 12273–7.

13. G.I. Fokina et al. [Experimental phytotherapy of tick-born encephalitis.] *Voprosy Virusologii* 36, no. 1(1991): 18–21.

14. R.S. Taylor et al. Antiviral activities of Nepalese medicinal plants. *Journal of Ethnopharmacology* 52, no. 3 (1996): 157–63.

15. M. Castleman. *The Healing Herbs* (Melbourne, Australia: Schwartz Books, 1991), pp. 321–25.

16. V.E. Guseinova et al. [Examining the antimicrobial properties of medicinal plant species.] *Farmatsiya* 41(4) (1992): 21–4.

17. E.L. Avenirova. [Effect of novoimanine on the cellular permeability indices of staphylococci.] *Antibiotiki* 22, no. 7 (1977): 630–4.

18. A.I. Gurevich et al. [Antibiotic hyperforin from Hypericum perforatum L.] *Antibiotiki* 16, no. 6(1971): 510–3.

19. V.A. Molochko et al. [The antistaphylococcal properties of plant extracts in relation to their prospective use as therapeutic and prophylactic formulations for the skin.] *Vestnik Dermatogii I Venerologii,* no. 8(1990): 54–6.

20. N.S. Zakharova et al. [Action of plant extracts on the natural immunity indices of animals.] *Zhurnal Mikrobiologii, Epidemiologii I Immunobiologii,* no. 4(1986): 71–5.

21. A.G. Kolesnikova. [Bactericidal and immunocorrective properties of plant extracts.] *Zhurnal Mikrobiologii, Epidemiologii I Immunobiologii,* no. 3(1986): 75–8.

22. See 18.

23. M.I. Davidov, V.G. Goriunov, and P.G. Kubarikov. [Phytoperfusion of the bladder after adenomectomy.] *Urologiia I Nefrologiia (Moskva),* no. 5(1995): 19–20.

24. See 21.

25. T.A. Evstifeeva and S.V. Sibiriak. [The immunotropic properties of biologically active products obtained from Klamath weed (Hypericum perforatum L.).] *Eksperimentalnaia I Klinicheskaia Farmakologiia* 59, no. 1(1996): 51–4.

26. T. Shipochliev, A. Dimitrov, and E. Aleksandrova. [Anti-inflammatory action of a group of plant extracts.] *Veterinarno-Meditenski Nauki* 18, no. 6(1981): 87–94.

27. R. Melzer, U. Fricke, and J. Holzl. Vasoactive properties of procyanidins from Hypericum perforatum L. in isolated porcine coronary arteries. *Arzneimittel-Forschung* 41, no. 5(1991): 481–3.

28. W.T. Couldwell et al. Hypericin: a potential antiglioma therapy. *Neurosurgery* 35, no. 4(1994): 705–10.

29. A.L. Vandenbogaerde et al. Antitumor activity of photosensitized hypericin on A431 cell xenografts. *Anticancer Research* 16, no. 4A(1996): 1619–25.

30. Q.M. VanderWerf et al. Hypericin: a new laser phototargeting agent for human cancer cells. *Laryngoscope* 106, no. 4(1996): 479–83.

31. C. Thomas and R.S. Pardini. Oxygen dependence of hypericin-induced phototoxicity to EMT6 mouse mammary carcinoma cells. *Photochemistry and Photobiology* 55, no. 6(1992): 831–7.

32. B. Vukovic-Gacic and D. Simic. Identification of natural antimutagens with modulating effects on DNA repair. *Basic Life Sciences* 61(1993): 269–77.

33. A.V. Smyshliaeva and IuB. Kudriashov. [The modification of a radiation lesion with an aqueous extract of Hypericum perforatum L.] *Biologicheskie Nauki*, no. 4(1992): 7–9.

Chapter 5. Why Doctors Are Still Stuck on Toxic Drugs

1. H. Woelk, G. Burkard, and J. Grunwald. Benefits and risks of the hypericum extract LI 160: drug monitoring study with 3250 patients. *Journal of Geriatric Psychiatry and Neurology* 7 Suppl. 1(1994): S 34–8.

2. A. Weil. *Health and Healing* (Boston: Houghton Mifflin, 1983): 99–102.

3. G. Harrer and V. Schulz. Clinical investigation of the anti-depressant effectiveness of hypericum. *Journal of Geriatric Psychiatry and Neurology* 7 Suppl. 1(1994): S 6–8.

4. L. Yip et al. Antiviral activity of a derivative of the photo-sensitive compound hypericin. *Phytomedicine* 3, no. 2(1996): 185–190.

Chapter 6. Is St. John's Wort for You?

1. A.T. Beck and A.J. Rush. Cognitive therapy. In: H.I. Kaplan and B.J. Sadock, eds. *Comprehensive Textbook of Psychiatry VI*, vol. 2, 6th ed. (Baltimore: Williams and Wilkins, 1995): 1847–57.

Chapter 8. How to Use St. John's Wort

1. R. Kerb et al. Single-dose and steady-state pharmacoki-netics of hypericin and pseudohypericin. *Antimicrobial Agents and Chemotherapy* 40, no. 9(1996): 2087–93.

Chapter 9. The Side Effects—They're Rare, But They Do Occur

1. H. Woelk, G. Burkard, and J. Grunwald. Benefits and risks of the hypericum extract LI 160: drug monitoring study

with 3250 patients. *Journal of Geriatric Psychiatry and Neurology* 7 Suppl. 1(1994): S 34–8.

2. B. Witte et al. [Treatment of depressive symptoms with a high concentration hypericum preparation. A multicenter placebo-controlled double-blind study.] *Fortschritte Der Medizin* 113, no. 28(1995): 404–8.

3. H. Sommer and G. Harrer. Placebo-controlled double-blind study examining the effectiveness of an hypericum preparation in 105 mildly depressed patients. *Journal of Geriatric Psychiatry and Neurology* 7 Suppl. 1(1994): S 9–11.

4. E.U. Vorbach, W.D. Hubner, and K.H. Arnoldt. Effectiveness and tolerance of the hypericum extract LI 160 in comparison with imipramine: randomized double-blind study with 135 outpatients. *Journal of Geriatric Psychiatry and Neurology* 7 Suppl. 1(1994): S 19–23.

5. K. Linde et al. St. John's wort for depression—an overview and meta-analysis of randomised clinical trials. *British Medical Journal* 313, no. 7052(1996): 253–8.

6. See 1.

7. R. Kerb et al. No clinically relevant photosensitization after single-dose and steady-state treatment with Hypericum extract in man. *European Journal of Clinical Pharmacology* 49, nos. 1–2(1995): A156.

8. See 1.

9. Ibid.

10. H.I. Kaplan, B.J. Sadock, and J.A. Grebb. *Kaplan and Sadock's Synopsis of Psychiatry,* 7th ed. (Baltimore: Williams and Wilkins, 1994), 978.

11. See 1.

12. See 4.

13. See 1.

Chapter 11. The Earth's Own Medicine

1. R.C.H. Shepherd. A Canadian isolate of Colletotrichum gloeosporoides as a potential biological control agent for St. John's wort (Hypericum perforatum) in Australia. *Plant Protection Quarterly* 10, no. 4(1995): 148–151.

2. D.T. Briese and P.W. Jupp. Establishment, spread, and initial impact of Aphis chloric Koch (Hemiptera: Aphididae) introduced into Australia for the biological control of St. John's wort. *Biocontrol Science and Technology* 5, no. 3(1995): 271–285.

3. R. Van den Bosch, P.S. Messenger, and A.P. Gutierrez. *An Introduction to Biological Control* (New York: Plenum Press, 1982).

4. Ibid.

5. Ibid.

INDEX

About the Author

Jonathan Zuess, M.D., is a physician who has trained in both conventional and alternative medicines. His interest in natural medicine is a family tradition, stretching back many generations. After completing medical school and doing an internship in conventional medicine and a residency in psychiatry, he studied a number of alternative therapies. He is a member of the American Holistic Medical Association. He is also an avid backpacker and has spent several months exploring remote wilderness areas in Australia. He practices in Arizona, where he is working on his next book, *The Wisdom of Depression,* a comprehensive, holistic guide to the treatment of depression.